T0284749

Printed in the USA
CPSIA information can be obtained
at www.ICGtesting.com
JSHW011350130824
68072JS00010B/212

9 780874 416756

THE NEW AMERICAN
HAGGADAH

הַגָּדָה שֶׁל פֶּסַח

Developed by Rabbi Mordecai M. Kaplan,
Rabbi Eugene Kohn, and Rabbi Ira Eisenstein
for the Jewish Reconstructionist Foundation

Edited by Gila Gevirtz

Editorial Committee

Rabbi Nina Beth Cardin   Rabbi William Cutter
Rabbi Laura Geller   Rabbi Richard Hirsh
Rabbi Allan Lehmann   Rabbi Julie Schonfeld
Rabbi Sidney Schwarz

BEHRMAN HOUSE, INC.

Cover and Book Design: Irving S. Berman

We are grateful to the publishers and authors listed below for having kindly granted us permission to print the following material:

Excerpt from *Our Passover Haggadah,* copyright © 1994 by Arlene and Charles Silberman

Excerpt from "Out of Africa: An Ethiopian Woman's Exodus," originally published in *Lilith, The Independent Jewish Feminist Magazine,* Volume 18, No.2.

"Miriam's Song" from *And You Shall Be a Blessing;* music and lyrics by Debbie Friedman; lyrics based on Exodus 15:20–21; copyright © 1988 by Deborah Lynn Friedman (ASCAP), Sounds Write Productions, Inc. (ASCAP)

"B'chol Dor Vador," music and lyrics copyright © 1998 by Linda Hirschhorn

We gratefully acknowledge the cooperation of the following sources of photographs and art for this book:

American Jewish Historical Society, 33 (right), 59; Creative Image Photography, cover (center), v, vi, vii, viii, 12, 13, 29, 51, 103; Gustov Doré, 20, 21, 22, 23, 24, 25, 26, 27, 28, 29, 30; Gila Gevirtz, 17, 19, 104; The Greater New York Conference on Soviet Jewry, 33 (left); International Ladies Garment Workers Union Archives, 44, 45; Israel Ministry of Tourism, 8, 94, 95; Jewish Theological Seminary, 36; Jewish Theological Seminary, Joseph and Miriam Ratner Center for the Study of Conservative Judaism, 46, 47; The Jewish Museum, 3 (center); Francene Keery, vi (center, 1995), 14 (1996), 61 (1996); New Israel Fund/Debbi Cooper, 66, 67; Mark Newman/SuperStock, 80, 81; Joan Roth, 31; Clare Sieffert, 2, 6, 7, 46, 52, 53, 64, 65, 68, 69, 76, 77, 101; Jean Speiser/UNICEF, 96, 97, 98, 99, 100; Leonard Weisgard, 40, 76; YIVO Institute for Jewish Research, 71 (bottom right).

© Copyright 1941, 1978, 1999 by Behrman House, Inc.

Library of Congress Cataloging-in-Publication Data

Haggadah (Reconstructionist). English & Hebrew.
    The New American Haggadah/developed by Mordecai M. Kaplan, Eugene Kohn, and Ira Eisenstein for the Jewish Reconstructionist Foundation; edited by Gila Gevirtz. — [Rev. ed.]
    p.   cm.
    Rev. ed. of: The New Haggadah for the Pesaḥ Seder
    ISBN 978-0-87441-675-6
    1. Haggadot—Texts.   2. Seder—Liturgy—Texts.   3. Reconstructionist Judaism—Liturgy—Texts.   I. Kaplan, Mordecai Menahem   II. Kohn, Eugene III. Eisenstein, Ira   IV. Gevirtz, Gila   V. Jewish Reconstructionist Foundation. VI. Title.
    BM674.73J49   1999
    296.4'5371048—dc21   98-43136
                                                                CIP
                                                                HE

Manufactured in the United States of America

INTRODUCTION

Every year, on the 15th day of the Jewish month of Nisan, we are urged not only to retell but also to embellish the story of the Exodus. The more we do so, we are told in the Passover Haggadah, the more we are to be praised. Such was the standard set by the ancient rabbis, and such was the teaching of Rabbi Mordecai Kaplan *(z"l)*.

It was Rabbi Kaplan's conviction that Judaism acquires its authenticity by evolving in response to the changing conditions that confront the Jewish community. He further asserted that—the importance of Israel notwithstanding—a thriving Diaspora is essential for the creative survival of Judaism. In 1941, Rabbi Kaplan produced a groundbreaking work—*The New Haggadah*—with Rabbis Eugene Kohn and Ira Eisenstein. They revised it in 1978. Now we have revised it again and renamed it *The New American Haggadah.*

In earlier editions, Kaplan and his co-editors noted, "We have retained the traditional framework [of the Haggadah], with its [classic] charm, but we have filled it in with the...content of present-day idealism and aspiration." In the process, the editors omitted passages that, in their words, "convey no special message" or "might conflict with our own highest ethical standards." For example, they omitted the rabbinic musings that multiplied the number of plagues and edited the hymn Dayeinu. Among the readings they added were "Pharaoh, Arch-Tyrant," the Moses legends, and the verses from the Torah that emphasize the ethical implications of the Exodus.

Together, these changes were designed to inspire in the new generation the same devotion to freedom that our ancestors gained from the ancient Haggadah. The goal of *The New American Haggadah* remains the same.

Thus, the 15 steps of the seder—as they traditionally have been defined and sequenced—remain the sturdy loom upon which the evening's tapestry is woven. And the Passover vision of freedom, justice, and peace has been shaped by interweaving the threads of ancient Jewish tradition with the creative and ethical legacy of the modern American Diaspora.

In the spirit of Rabbis Kaplan, Kohn, and Eisenstein, we have edited those features that are at odds with the sensibilities and circumstances of our time. For example, we have edited the English text so that it is gender inclusive and shortened the Hallel to enable participants to complete the full order of the seder.

Among the additions that have been made are references to the matriarchs in the Hebrew and Aramaic text, music by Jewish-American songwriters, riddles to engage children, a memoir written by a Union soldier celebrating Passover during the American Civil War, and a modern exodus story recounted by an Ethiopian Jew. All the illustrations in the Haggadah are new, and many reflect the diverse ways American Jews have enriched the Passover message of liberation.

As was true in earlier editions, the English version of the text is in large measure paraphrase. However, where a literal translation of the Hebrew is provided, it is in part original and in part derived from published translations of the Bible.

Revising *The New Haggadah* has been an exciting challenge. It called upon us to transmit our tradition even as we reinvented it. Such are the challenges passed on to us by Mordecai Kaplan. We believe that *The New American Haggadah* would have pleased Rabbi Kaplan and hope that you, your family, and your friends will find joy, inspiration, and renewal in it.

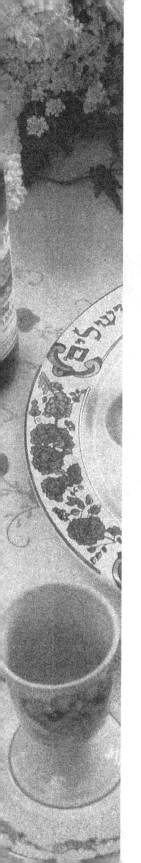

THE SEDER TABLE

The seder table should delight the senses. Holiday candles add a beautiful glow, and a white tablecloth and fragrant bouquet of flowers can add to the beauty of the service. The seder table also includes an array of symbolic objects:

THREE MATZOT are placed separately in the three sections of a ritual matzah cover, or in the folds of an ordinary napkin. Two matzot symbolize the two loaves of bread over which the usual benediction is recited on Shabbat and festivals. The third matzah emphasizes the role of matzah in the Passover ritual.

A ROASTED SHANKBONE commemorates the paschal sacrifice our ancestors brought to the Holy Temple on *Pesah*. The Talmud teaches that a beet, which bleeds when it is cut, may be used in place of the shankbone.

A ROASTED EGG symbolizes the festival sacrifice that was brought to the Temple and which, on Passover, supplemented the paschal lamb.

MAROR, the bitter herb, symbolizes the bitterness of Israel's bondage in Egypt. Horseradish is most often used as the maror.

HAROSET symbolizes the mortar the Israelites used in building the "treasure cities" for Pharaoh. Typically, it is a sweet paste made of fruits, nuts, spices, and wine or grape juice. Recipes for haroset abound in Jewish holiday cookbooks. Most are simple enough so that children can participate in their preparation.

Making the haroset

KARPAS, a vegetable—usually a green vegetable or a peeled boiled potato—is accompanied by a dish of salt water. The vegetable symbolizes the earth's renewal in spring and the sustaining hope of human redemption.

Place the shankbone, egg, maror, haroset, and vegetable on a seder plate in front of the person leading the seder, or at the center of the table if leadership is shared. (Some seder plates have hazeret, additional maror for the Hillel sandwhich.)

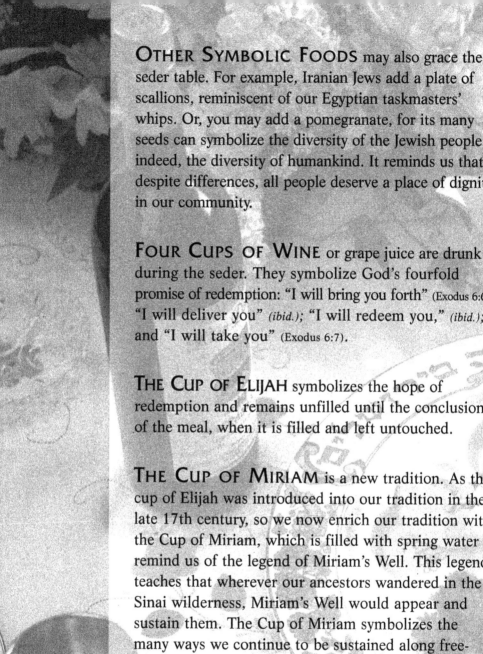

OTHER SYMBOLIC FOODS may also grace the seder table. For example, Iranian Jews add a plate of scallions, reminiscent of our Egyptian taskmasters' whips. Or, you may add a pomegranate, for its many seeds can symbolize the diversity of the Jewish people, indeed, the diversity of humankind. It reminds us that, despite differences, all people deserve a place of dignity in our community.

FOUR CUPS OF WINE or grape juice are drunk during the seder. They symbolize God's fourfold promise of redemption: "I will bring you forth" (Exodus 6:6); "I will deliver you" *(ibid.)*; "I will redeem you," *(ibid.)*; and "I will take you" (Exodus 6:7).

THE CUP OF ELIJAH symbolizes the hope of redemption and remains unfilled until the conclusion of the meal, when it is filled and left untouched.

THE CUP OF MIRIAM is a new tradition. As the cup of Elijah was introduced into our tradition in the late 17th century, so we now enrich our tradition with the Cup of Miriam, which is filled with spring water to remind us of the legend of Miriam's Well. This legend teaches that wherever our ancestors wandered in the Sinai wilderness, Miriam's Well would appear and sustain them. The Cup of Miriam symbolizes the many ways we continue to be sustained along freedom's path.

A PILLOW or cushioned armchair may be provided for the leader, and perhaps, for each person at the table, as a symbol of the comfort associated with freedom.

CANDLELIGHTING CEREMONY

Light the candles and recite the following benediction. When the seder service occurs on Shabbat, include the bracketed words.

Praised are you, Adonai our God, Sovereign of the universe, who sanctifies us through your mitzvot and commands us to light [Shabbat and] festival candles.

בָּרוּךְ אַתָּה יְיָ אֱלֹהֵינוּ מֶלֶךְ הָעוֹלָם,
אֲשֶׁר קִדְּשָׁנוּ בְּמִצְוֹתָיו וְצִוָּנוּ לְהַדְלִיק
נֵר שֶׁל [שַׁבָּת וְשֶׁל] יוֹם טוֹב.

Baruch atah adonai eloheinu, melech ha'olam, asher kid'shanu b'mitzvotav v'tzivanu l'hadlik ner shel [shabbat v'shel] yom tov.

THE ORDER
OF THE SERVICE

The ancient rabbis encouraged us to expand upon and renew the liturgy of the Haggadah at the same time that they prescribed a particular seder— meaning "order"— for the service. Thus, while each household's seder may vary in its details, the tradition asks us to journey through the night together, as our ancestors once did, by following the 15 steps outlined here.

קַדֵּשׁ	KADESH	*Recite Kiddush*
וּרְחַץ	UR'ḤATZ	*Wash the Hands*
כַּרְפַּס	KARPAS	*Dip the Vegetables*
יַחַץ	YAḤATZ	*Divide the Matzah*
מַגִּיד	MAGGID	*Tell the Passover Story*
רָחְצָה	ROḤTZAH	*Wash the Hands*
מוֹצִיא	MOTZI	*Recite the Motzi*
מַצָּה	MATZAH	*Eat the Matzah*
מָרוֹר	MAROR	*Eat the Maror*
כּוֹרֵךְ	KORECH	*Eat the Hillel Sandwich*
שֻׁלְחָן עוֹרֵךְ	SHULḤAN ORECH	*Eat the Festive Meal*
צָפוּן	TZAFUN	*Eat the Afikoman*
בָּרֵךְ	BARECH	*Give Thanks for the Meal*
הַלֵּל	HALLEL	*Sing Hymns of Praise*
נִרְצָה	NIRTZAH	*Complete the Seder*

INVOCATION

Raise the first cup of wine or grape juice and say:

Come, let us welcome the Passover!
May its constant renewal,
Spring after spring
In age after age
Recall our past and renew our potential,
For they are intertwined.
May tonight's celebration remind us
Of who we were, of who we are,
And of who we can become.

Descendants of slaves
We cannot fulfill tonight's obligation
Through ritual alone.
Reciting pious words
And eating symbolic foods
Will not suffice
To honor the Passover.
We are reminded this night
That we cannot truly be free
As long as others are enslaved.
The message our Haggadah proclaims
Is a song of universal freedom.

Excerpted from *Our Passover Haggadah,* a family Haggadah
by Charles and Arlene Silberman

REBELLION TO TYRANTS IS OBEDIENCE TO GOD.

Throughout history, the biblical story of the Exodus has been a symbol of and inspiration for the liberation of oppressed peoples. One design proposed in 1782 for the official seal of the United States illustrated the climactic moment of the Exodus story—the splitting of the Sea of Reeds and the escape of the children of Israel.

קַדֵּשׁ

When the seder service occurs on Shabbat, add the following paragraph:

וַיְהִי־עֶרֶב וַיְהִי־בֹקֶר יוֹם הַשִּׁשִּׁי: וַיְכֻלּוּ הַשָּׁמַיִם
וְהָאָרֶץ וְכָל־צְבָאָם: וַיְכַל אֱלֹהִים בַּיּוֹם הַשְּׁבִיעִי
מְלַאכְתּוֹ אֲשֶׁר עָשָׂה, וַיִּשְׁבֹּת בַּיּוֹם הַשְּׁבִיעִי
מִכָּל־מְלַאכְתּוֹ אֲשֶׁר עָשָׂה: וַיְבָרֶךְ אֱלֹהִים
אֶת־יוֹם הַשְּׁבִיעִי וַיְקַדֵּשׁ אֹתוֹ כִּי בוֹ שָׁבַת
מִכָּל־מְלַאכְתּוֹ אֲשֶׁר־בָּרָא אֱלֹהִים לַעֲשׂוֹת.

בָּרוּךְ אַתָּה יְיָ אֱלֹהֵינוּ מֶלֶךְ הָעוֹלָם,
בּוֹרֵא פְּרִי הַגָּפֶן:

Baruch atah adonai eloheinu, melech ha'olam,
borei pri hagafen.

On Shabbat, add the words in brackets:

בָּרוּךְ אַתָּה יְיָ אֱלֹהֵינוּ מֶלֶךְ הָעוֹלָם
אֲשֶׁר קִדְּשָׁנוּ בְּמִצְוֹתָיו, וַתִּתֶּן לָנוּ יְיָ
אֱלֹהֵינוּ בְּאַהֲבָה [שַׁבָּתוֹת לִמְנוּחָה וּ]
מוֹעֲדִים לְשִׂמְחָה חַגִּים וּזְמַנִּים
לְשָׂשׂוֹן אֶת־יוֹם [הַשַּׁבָּת הַזֶּה
וְאֶת־יוֹם] חַג הַמַּצּוֹת הַזֶּה זְמַן

KIDDUSH

When the seder service occurs on Shabbat, add the following paragraph:

There was evening, and there was morning, the sixth day. And the heavens and the earth and all their hosts were completed. And God, having finished the work by the seventh day, rested on the seventh day from all the work of Creation. And God blessed the seventh day, and hallowed it, resting from all the work of Creation. (Genesis 1:31–2:3)

Praised are you, Adonai our God, Sovereign of the universe, who creates the fruit of the vine.

On Shabbat, add the words in brackets:

Praised are you, Adonai our God, Sovereign of the universe, who sanctifies us through your commandments. As a token of your love, Eternal One our God, you have given us [Sabbaths for rest,] occasions for rejoicing, festivals and holidays for gladness, [this Shabbat and] this Feast of Unleavened Bread, the season of our liberation from bondage in Egypt. You quicken within us the desire to

חֵרוּתֵנוּ [בְּאַהֲבָה] מִקְרָא קֹדֶשׁ
זֵכֶר לִיצִיאַת מִצְרָיִם: כִּי אוֹתָנוּ
קֵרַבְתָּ לַעֲבוֹדָתֶךָ, [וְשַׁבָּת] וּמוֹעֲדֵי
קָדְשְׁךָ [בְּאַהֲבָה וּבְרָצוֹן] בְּשִׂמְחָה
וּבְשָׂשׂוֹן הִנְחַלְתָּנוּ. בָּרוּךְ אַתָּה יְיָ
מְקַדֵּשׁ [הַשַּׁבָּת וְ]יִשְׂרָאֵל וְהַזְּמַנִּים:

On Saturday night, add the following paragraph:

בָּרוּךְ אַתָּה יְיָ אֱלֹהֵינוּ מֶלֶךְ הָעוֹלָם, בּוֹרֵא
מְאוֹרֵי הָאֵשׁ: בָּרוּךְ אַתָּה יְיָ אֱלֹהֵינוּ מֶלֶךְ
הָעוֹלָם הַמַּבְדִּיל בֵּין קֹדֶשׁ לְחוֹל בֵּין אוֹר
לְחֹשֶׁךְ, בֵּין יוֹם הַשְּׁבִיעִי לְשֵׁשֶׁת יְמֵי־
הַמַּעֲשֶׂה. בֵּין קְדֻשַּׁת שַׁבָּת לִקְדֻשַּׁת יוֹם
טוֹב הִבְדַּלְתָּ, וְאֶת יוֹם הַשְּׁבִיעִי מִשֵּׁשֶׁת
יְמֵי הַמַּעֲשֶׂה קִדַּשְׁתָּ. בָּרוּךְ אַתָּה יְיָ
הַמַּבְדִּיל בֵּין קֹדֶשׁ לְקֹדֶשׁ:

בָּרוּךְ אַתָּה יְיָ אֱלֹהֵינוּ מֶלֶךְ הָעוֹלָם,
שֶׁהֶחֱיָנוּ וְקִיְּמָנוּ וְהִגִּיעָנוּ לַזְּמַן הַזֶּה:

Baruch atah adonai eloheinu, melech ha'olam,
sheheḥeyanu, v'kiy'manu, v'higi'anu
lazman hazeh.

Drink the first cup.

serve you, and [in love and grace], in joy and gladness, have bestowed on us your holy [Sabbaths and] festivals. Praised are you, Eternal One, who hallows [Shabbat,] Israel and the festivals.

These benedictions are a modified form of the havdalah ceremony performed at the end of Shabbat. The weekly ritual alludes to the distinction between the holiness of Shabbat and the weekdays. The benedictions that are recited when a festival immediately follows Shabbat affirm the distinction between the holiness of Shabbat and the holiness of the festival.

On Saturday night, add the following paragraph:

Praised are you, Adonai our God, Sovereign of the universe, who creates the light of fire.

Praised are you, Adonai our God, Sovereign of the universe, who distinguishes between the holy and the ordinary, between light and darkness, between the seventh day and the six days of work. You have distinguished between the holiness of Shabbat and the holiness of the festival and have hallowed the seventh day above the six days of work. Praised are you, Eternal One, who differentiates between the greater holiness and the lesser holiness.

Praised are you, Adonai our God, Sovereign of the universe, who has given us life, sustained us, and enabled us to reach this season.

Drink the first cup.

WASH THE HANDS וּרְחַץ

It is customary to wash the hands now, without reciting the usual benediction.

KARPAS כַּרְפַּס

Green vegetable or boiled potato, dipped in salt water, is distributed to all present, who say:

כִּי־הִנֵּה הַסְּתָו עָבָר. הַגֶּשֶׁם חָלַף הָלַךְ לוֹ:
הַנִּצָּנִים נִרְאוּ בָאָרֶץ עֵת הַזָּמִיר הִגִּיעַ.
וְקוֹל הַתּוֹר נִשְׁמַע בְּאַרְצֵנוּ:

(שִׁיר הַשִּׁירִים ב׳ י״א-י״ב)

Behold, winter is passed.
The rain has transformed the earth and vanished,
Buds now cover the earth and the time of singing has arrived,
The voice of the turtledove is heard in our land!

(Song of Songs 2:11–12)

These greens are a symbol of nature reborn. Before enjoying them, let us say together:

בָּרוּךְ אַתָּה יְיָ אֱלֹהֵינוּ מֶלֶךְ הָעוֹלָם, בּוֹרֵא
פְּרִי הָאֲדָמָה:

*Baruch atah adonai eloheinu, melech ha'olam,
borei pri ha'adamah.*

Praised are you, Adonai our God, Sovereign of the universe, who creates the fruit of the earth.

Both to enhance and facilitate the ritual washing of hands, bring a pitcher of water, a bowl, and a small towel to the table. One at a time, have the participants hold the bowl for the person next to them as that person pours water over his or her hands. Alternatively, one person can wash hands on behalf of all the participants.

You may want to set out a platter of vegetables to stave off the hunger pangs that can distract seder participants.

DIVIDE THE MATZAH יַחַץ

This Israeli stamp shows one of Marc Chagall's famous stained-glass windows commissioned for the Hadassah Hospital in Jerusalem. The Hadassah Medical Organization has served as a bridge to peace and understanding by treating thousands of Christians and Muslims from neighboring Arab countries.

Let us remember the teaching of the sage, Rabbi Tarfon: "It is not your duty to complete the work; neither are you free to cease from it." As you move through the service, discuss the steps you can take—individually and with the community—to fulfill your commitment to Israel and to freedom, justice, and prosperity for all humankind.

The leader breaks the middle matzah in two, returning the smaller part to the middle, and wrapping the larger part (the afikoman). Raising the afikoman, the leader says:

We will now hide the afikoman as a reminder that although the process of redemption began with the Exodus, part remains hidden. After dinner, we will share the afikoman, so that we may savor the taste of redemption and be reminded to do our share to bring about a better world.

After the afikoman is hidden, the children are challenged to find and then hide it. (Alternatively, the leader places it in a public place, and the children try to "steal" and hide it.) The leader redeems the afikoman after dinner in exchange for the promise of gifts.

The leader raises the matzah and says:

הָא לַחְמָא עַנְיָא דִי אֲכָלוּ אַבְהָתָנָא
וְאִמְהָתָנָא בְּאַרְעָא דְמִצְרָיִם. כָּל־דִּכְפִין
יֵיתֵי וְיֵיכָל, כָּל־דִּצְרִיךְ יֵיתֵי וְיִפְסַח. הָשַׁתָּא
הָכָא, לְשָׁנָה הַבָּאָה בְּאַרְעָא דְיִשְׂרָאֵל.
הָשַׁתָּא עַבְדֵי, לְשָׁנָה הַבָּאָה בְּנֵי חוֹרִין:

This is the matzah, symbol of the bread of poverty, which our ancestors ate in the land of Egypt! Let it remind us to respond to the many people today who are hungry and poor. Whoever is hungry—let them come and eat! Whoever is in need—let them come and celebrate Passover!

Let us strive unceasingly for that day when all will share equally in the joy of Passover—when the land of Israel will be built up in peace, and all humanity will enjoy the fruits of freedom, justice, and prosperity.

At the base of the Statue of Liberty is a sonnet written by the Jewish poet and social activist Emma Lazarus. Her words bring to mind the Passover vision of God's outstretched arm leading us toward liberation: "Give me your tired, your poor, your huddled masses yearning to breathe free."

LET MY PEOPLE GO

Tonight's festival is dedicated to the dream and the hope of freedom, the dream and the hope that have filled the hearts of humankind from the time our ancestors went forth out of Egypt. Peoples have suffered and nations have struggled to make this dream come true. Now we rededicate ourselves to the struggle for freedom. Though the sacrifice be great and the hardships many, we will not rest until the chains that enslave all peoples are broken.

But the freedom we strive for means more than broken chains. It means liberation from all those enslavements that warp the spirit and blight the mind, that destroy the soul even though they leave the flesh alive. For humanity can be enslaved in more ways than one.

People can be enslaved to themselves. When they let emotion sway them to hurt, and when they permit harmful habits to tyrannize them—they are slaves. When laziness or cowardice keeps them from doing what they know to be right, and when ignorance blinds them to the suffering of others—they are slaves. When envy, bitterness, and jealousy sour their joys and diminish the glow of their contentment—they are slaves, shackled by chains of their own forging.

People can be enslaved by poverty and inequality. When the fear of need drives them to dishonesty and violence, to defending the guilty and accusing the innocent—they are slaves. When the work people do enriches others but leaves them and their children without safe housing, warm clothes, and nourishing food—they are slaves.

People can be enslaved by intolerance. When Jews are forced to abandon their Torah, to neglect their sacred festivals, to leave off rebuilding their ancient homeland—they are slaves. When the poor, aged, or ailing are derided and attacked—they are slaves. When women, men, or children live in fear of hatred and prejudice—they are slaves.

How deeply these enslavements have scarred the world! The wars, the destruction, the suffering, the waste! Passover calls us to be free—free from the tyranny of our own selves, free from the enslavement of poverty and inequality, free from the hate that corrodes the ties uniting the family of humankind.

Passover calls upon us to end all slavery. Passover cries out in the name of God, "Let my people go!"

The Hebrew word for Egypt is *mitzrayim*. It comes from the same root as *tzar*, meaning "narrow." When we are enslaved by our feelings and desires, we live in a *mitzrayim* of our own making. It is a narrow place from which we cannot clearly see ourselves or the needs of others.

From childho
we are each
asked to
participate ir
the tradition
that has bee
passed on tc
us from Mos
Miriam, and
Aaron.

THE FOUR QUESTIONS
מַה נִּשְׁתַּנָּה

The youngest child present asks the following questions:

How different this night of Passover is from all other
nights of the year!

מַה נִּשְׁתַּנָּה הַלַּיְלָה הַזֶּה מִכָּל־הַלֵּילוֹת,

Mah nishtanah halailah hazeh mikol haleilot:

On all other nights, we eat either leavened or unleavened
bread; *why, on this night, do we eat only matzah,
unleavened bread?*

שֶׁבְּכָל־הַלֵּילוֹת אָנוּ אוֹכְלִין חָמֵץ וּמַצָּה,
הַלַּיְלָה הַזֶּה כֻּלּוֹ מַצָּה:

*Sheb'chol haleilot anu ochlin hametz umatzah, halailah
hazeh kulo matzah.*

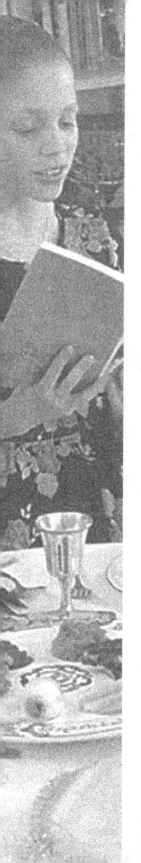

On all other nights, we eat vegetables and herbs of all kinds; *why, on this night, must we specifically eat maror?*

שֶׁבְּכָל־הַלֵּילוֹת אָנוּ אוֹכְלִין שְׁאָר יְרָקוֹת, הַלַּיְלָה הַזֶּה מָרוֹר:

Sheb'chol haleilot anu ochlin sh'ar y'rakot, halailah hazeh maror.

On all other nights, we do not necessarily dip greens in water or in anything else; *why, on this night, do we dip the karpas in salt water and the maror in ḥaroset?*

שֶׁבְּכָל־הַלֵּילוֹת אֵין אָנוּ מַטְבִּילִין אֲפִילוּ פַּעַם אֶחָת, הַלַּיְלָה הַזֶּה שְׁתֵּי פְעָמִים:

Sheb'chol haleilot ein anu mat'bilin afilu pa'am eḥat, halailah hazeh sh'tei f'amim.

On all other nights, everyone sits up straight at the table; *why, on this night, do we recline at the table?*

שֶׁבְּכָל־הַלֵּילוֹת אָנוּ אוֹכְלִין בֵּין יוֹשְׁבִין וּבֵין מְסֻבִּין, הַלַּיְלָה הַזֶּה כֻּלָּנוּ מְסֻבִּין:

Sheb'chol haleilot anu ochlin bein yoshvin uvein m'subin, halailah hazeh kulanu m'subin.

The karpas symbolizes the earth's regeneration in spring.

THE STORY   מַגִּיד

The leader replies to the child:

Indeed, this night *is* very different from all the other nights of the year, for on this night we celebrate one of the most important moments in the history of our people. On this night, we celebrate our going forth in triumph from slavery into freedom.

On this night, too, we retell our people's story. But even before the telling begins, we can answer these four questions in a few short words.

WHY DO WE EAT ONLY MATZAH TONIGHT?
When Pharaoh let our ancestors go from Egypt, they were forced to flee in great haste. With not a moment to spare, they snatched up the dough they had prepared and fled. But the hot sun beat down as they carried the dough along with them and baked it into a flat, unleavened bread they called matzah. To remember this event, we eat only matzah on Passover.

WHY DO WE EAT BITTER HERBS ON PASSOVER NIGHT?

We eat maror to remind us how bitter our ancestors' lives were made by their enslavement in Egypt.

WHY DO WE DIP TWICE TONIGHT?

You have already heard that we dip the karpas in salt water because it reminds us of the green that shoots forth from the earth in springtime. We dip the maror in the sweet haroset as a sign of hope; our ancestors were able to withstand the bitterness of slavery because it was sweetened by the hope of freedom.

The haroset also reminds us of the mortar the Israelites used to build the cities of Pithom and Ramses.

WHY DO WE RECLINE AT THE TABLE?

Reclining at the table was a sign of being a free person in ancient times. Because our ancestors were freed on this night, we recline at the table.

Now let us recite the story of Passover as we find it in the Torah and in the writings of the ancient rabbis.

עֲבָדִים הָיִינוּ לְפַרְעֹה בְּמִצְרַיִם, וַיּוֹצִיאֵנוּ
יְיָ אֱלֹהֵינוּ מִשָּׁם בְּיָד חֲזָקָה וּבִזְרוֹעַ נְטוּיָה.
וְאִלּוּ לֹא הוֹצִיא הַקָּדוֹשׁ בָּרוּךְ הוּא אֶת־
אֲבוֹתֵינוּ וְאֶת־אִמּוֹתֵינוּ מִמִּצְרַיִם, הֲרֵי אָנוּ
וּבָנֵינוּ וּבְנֵי בָנֵינוּ מְשֻׁעְבָּדִים הָיִינוּ לְפַרְעֹה
בְּמִצְרָיִם. וַאֲפִילוּ כֻּלָּנוּ חֲכָמִים, כֻּלָּנוּ נְבוֹנִים,
כֻּלָּנוּ זְקֵנִים, כֻּלָּנוּ יוֹדְעִים אֶת־הַתּוֹרָה,
מִצְוָה עָלֵינוּ לְסַפֵּר בִּיצִיאַת מִצְרָיִם.
וְכָל־הַמַּרְבֶּה לְסַפֵּר בִּיצִיאַת מִצְרַיִם הֲרֵי
זֶה מְשֻׁבָּח:

Avadim hayinu l'faroh b'mitzrayim, vayotzi'einu adonai eloheinu misham b'yad hazakah uvizro'a n'tuyah.

Once we were slaves to Pharaoh in Egypt, but the Eternal One our God brought us forth with a strong hand and an outstretched arm. If God had not brought our ancestors out of Egypt, we and our children and our children's children might still be enslaved. Therefore, even if we all were wise, even if we all were insightful and learned in the Torah, it would still be our duty to tell and retell the story of the Exodus from Egypt. The more we reflect upon the story, the deeper will be our understanding of what freedom means, and the stronger our determination to win it for ourselves and for others.

The rabbis of long ago loved to tell and retell the story of Passover. Once five rabbis became so engrossed in talking together about the freeing of the Israelites that they stayed up all night. The story is told:

מַעֲשֶׂה בְּרַבִּי אֱלִיעֶזֶר וְרַבִּי יְהוֹשֻׁעַ וְרַבִּי
אֶלְעָזָר בֶּן־עֲזַרְיָה וְרַבִּי עֲקִיבָא וְרַבִּי טַרְפוֹן
שֶׁהָיוּ מְסֻבִּין בִּבְנֵי בְרַק. וְהָיוּ מְסַפְּרִים
בִּיצִיאַת מִצְרַיִם כָּל־אֹתוֹ הַלַּיְלָה, עַד
שֶׁבָּאוּ תַלְמִידֵיהֶם וְאָמְרוּ לָהֶם, רַבּוֹתֵינוּ
הִגִּיעַ זְמַן קְרִיאַת שְׁמַע שֶׁל שַׁחֲרִית:

It happened that Rabbi Eliezer, and Rabbi Joshua, and Rabbi Elazar ben Azariah, and Rabbi Akiva and Rabbi Tarfon were feasting together in the village of B'nai B'rak, and they talked about the Exodus from Egypt for such a long time that, before they knew it, their students were calling to them, "The dawn is here; it is time to recite the morning Sh'ma."

בָּרוּךְ הַמָּקוֹם בָּרוּךְ הוּא. בָּרוּךְ שֶׁנָּתַן
תּוֹרָה לְעַמּוֹ יִשְׂרָאֵל, בָּרוּךְ הוּא: כְּנֶגֶד
אַרְבָּעָה בָנִים דִּבְּרָה תוֹרָה, אֶחָד חָכָם, וְאֶחָד
רָשָׁע, וְאֶחָד תָּם, וְאֶחָד שֶׁאֵינוֹ יוֹדֵעַ לִשְׁאוֹל:

It has been suggested that these rabbis were planning the Bar Kochba Revolt (132–135 CE [Common Era]) against their Roman oppressors. Indeed, the word sh'ma, which means "hearken" and is the first word of the primary declaration of the Jewish faith, may have been a password to warn them of the enemy's approach.

— 16 —

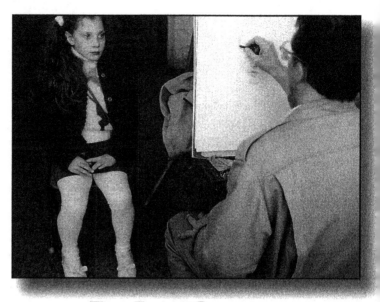

THE FOUR CHILDREN

Thus the story of the Exodus was told and retold, from generation to generation; parents would tell the story to their children, so that they, in turn, might tell it to their children. But, as the ancient rabbis knew, children are different from one another. And so, they spoke of four kinds of children and how to respond most effectively to each one.

The rabbis found in the Torah four versions of the command to tell the story of the Exodus to our children. From this, they inferred that there were four kinds of children, four different ways of responding to our Jewish heritage.

THE FIRST KIND OF CHILD IS THE WISE CHILD.

The wise child loves Passover and is eager to celebrate the holiday. This child asks, "'What are the decrees, the statutes, and the laws that the Eternal One our God has commanded' concerning Passover?" (Deuteronomy 6:20) Teach this child the customs and rituals of the festival. Reveal their beauty, not only as beloved traditions but also as the symbols of a noble ideal—the ideal of freedom for all people.

חָכָם מָה הוּא אוֹמֵר: מָה הָעֵדֹת וְהַחֻקִּים
וְהַמִּשְׁפָּטִים אֲשֶׁר צִוָּה יְיָ אֱלֹהֵינוּ אֶתְכֶם:
(דברים ו כ) וְאַף אַתָּה אֱמָר־לוֹ כְּהִלְכוֹת
הַפֶּסַח: אֵין מַפְטִירִין אַחַר הַפֶּסַח אֲפִיקוֹמָן:

ANOTHER KIND OF CHILD IS THE IRREVERENT CHILD.
The irreverent child is scornful, detached from the
celebration and the community. This child asks, "What
does this service mean to *you?*" speaking as an outsider.
(Exodus 12:26) Scold this child saying, "'It is because of what
God did for me when I went out of Egypt.' (Exodus 13:8)
For me; not for you; for a commitment to the community
must be made before enjoying the blessings bestowed
upon the community. Because you set yourself apart
from the Jewish people, you would not have made the
journey from slavery to freedom."

רָשָׁע מָה הוּא אוֹמֵר: מָה הָעֲבֹדָה הַזֹּאת
לָכֶם: (שמות י"ב כ"ו) לָכֶם וְלֹא לוֹ. וּלְפִי
שֶׁהוֹצִיא אֶת־עַצְמוֹ מִן הַכְּלָל כָּפַר בָּעִקָּר.
וְאַף אַתָּה הַקְהֵה אֶת־שִׁנָּיו וֶאֱמָר־לוֹ: בַּעֲבוּר
זֶה עָשָׂה יְיָ לִי בְּצֵאתִי מִמִּצְרָיִם: (שמות י"ג ח)
לִי וְלֹא לוֹ. אִלּוּ הָיָה שָׁם, לֹא הָיָה נִגְאָל:

THE THIRD KIND OF CHILD IS THE SIMPLE CHILD.
The simple child is naïve and innocent, and very shy.
This child would like to know what Passover means
but cannot formulate sophisticated questions. The
simple child asks, "What is this all about?" (Exodus 13:14)
Reassure this youngster, "With a strong hand, God
brought us forth from Egypt, out of the house of
bondage."

תָּם מָה הוּא אוֹמֵר: מַה־זֹּאת, וְאָמַרְתָּ אֵלָיו,
בְּחֹזֶק יָד הוֹצִיאָנוּ יְיָ מִמִּצְרַיִם מִבֵּית
עֲבָדִים: (שמות י"ג י"ד)

AND THE FOURTH KIND OF CHILD IS THE ONE WHO DOES NOT REALIZE THAT SOMETHING UNUSUAL IS GOING ON. Awaken this child saying, "'This is because of what God did for me when I went forth from Egypt.'"

(Exodus 13:8)

וְשֶׁאֵינוֹ יוֹדֵעַ לִשְׁאוֹל אַתְּ פְּתַח לוֹ. שֶׁנֶּאֱמַר,
וְהִגַּדְתָּ לְבִנְךָ בַּיּוֹם הַהוּא לֵאמֹר, בַּעֲבוּר זֶה
עָשָׂה יְיָ לִי בְּצֵאתִי מִמִּצְרָיִם: (שמות י"ג ח)

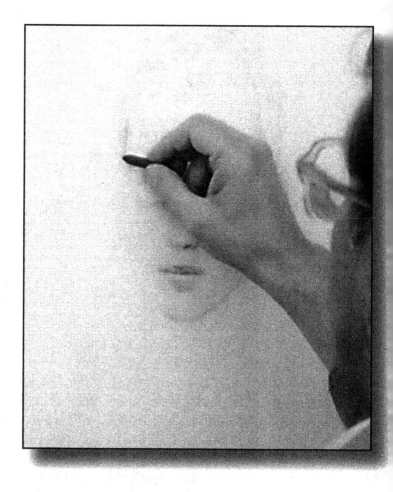

The four children can be understood as four traits within each of us. If your portrait were drawn tonight, which child might it reflect?
If a fifth child were added to the Haggadah, what trait might that child represent? What question might the fifth child ask?

Jacob arrives in Egypt.

מִתְּחִלָּה עוֹבְדֵי עֲבוֹדָה זָרָה הָיוּ אֲבוֹתֵינוּ
וְאִמּוֹתֵינוּ, וְעַכְשָׁו קֵרְבָנוּ הַמָּקוֹם לַעֲבוֹדָתוֹ.

In the beginning, our ancestors worshipped idols,
but then God embraced us so that we might better
serve God.

HOW ISRAEL CAME TO EGYPT

The Torah tells us that God commanded Abraham to leave
Mesopotamia and his father Terah's house and go to the
land of Canaan, where he would become the founder of "a
great nation." (Genesis 12:2) Abraham obeyed God's command
and journeyed with his wife, Sarah, to Canaan. There God
blessed them. A child, Isaac, was born to them; and to Isaac
and his wife, Rebecca, were born Esau and Jacob. Jacob
later became known as Yisrael, and went down to Egypt
with his family.

Why did Jacob go down to Egypt? Because his son Joseph had become prime minister to Pharaoh, king of Egypt. When a famine broke out in Canaan, Joseph asked his father and all his family to join him there. The book of Deuteronomy tells about this too: "My father was a wandering Aramean. He went down to Egypt with just a few people and sojourned there. Before long, however, the few became a nation, great, mighty, and numerous." (Deuteronomy 26:5)

But soon a "new king arose over Egypt who knew not Joseph," and he enslaved the Israelites, the descendants of Jacob. (Exodus 1:8) God had warned Abraham that this would happen. God had said: "Know that your descendants will be strangers in a land not their own. There they will be enslaved and oppressed for four hundred years." (Genesis 15: 13) But God had also promised Abraham that his descendants would later go free, saying, "The very nation they will serve, will I bring to judgment, and they [the Israelites] will go forth with great wealth." (Genesis 15:14) Thus the Israelites were to learn what it means to be slaves; thus they were to be made ready for the sacred role they were destined to play as defenders of justice and freedom.

While in Egypt, the Israelites kept faith with God, remembering God's promise to their ancestors. They held fast to their ways, keeping ever faithful to the covenant. And God kept faith with Israel. God redeemed the promise and delivered them. Tonight, we celebrate the everlasting covenant of faith binding God and the Jewish people as one.

The Torah also tells us of Ishmael, who was born to Abraham and Sarah's hand-maiden, Hagar, and of whom God promises, "I will make a great nation of him." (Genesis 21:18) Ishmael became the progenitor of Islam; and thus, Abraham is regarded as a patriarch by two great traditions.

וְהִיא שֶׁעָמְדָה לַאֲבוֹתֵינוּ וּלְאִמּוֹתֵינוּ וְלָנוּ,
שֶׁלֹּא אֶחָד בִּלְבַד עָמַד עָלֵינוּ לְכַלּוֹתֵנוּ,
אֶלָּא שֶׁבְּכָל־דּוֹר וָדוֹר עוֹמְדִים עָלֵינוּ
לְכַלּוֹתֵנוּ, וְהַקָּדוֹשׁ־בָּרוּךְ־הוּא מַצִּילֵנוּ
מִיָּדָם:

*Vehi she'amdah la'avoteinu ul'imoteinu v'lanu, shelo
ehad bilvad amad aleinu l'chaloteinu, ela sheb'chol dor
vador omdim aleinu l'chaloteinu, v'hakadosh baruch hu
matzileinu miyadam.*

God's faithfulness to Israel has ever been a source of
strength to our ancestors and to us. For not only the
Egyptians rose up to destroy us—in every generation
do our enemies rise up against us, and God delivers
us from their hands.

Moses is found by Pharaoh's daughter.

THE SUFFERING OF ISRAEL IN EGYPT

The new king said to his advisers, "'Look, the Israelites are too many and too mighty for us. We must deal wisely with them, lest they multiply and, should we be at war, join our enemies and fight against us.' So Pharaoh set taskmasters over them to crush them with heavy loads; and they built for Pharaoh the treasure cities of Pithom and Ramses. . . . The Egyptians forced the Israelites to serve with crushing labor." (Exodus 1:9–11, 13)

וַיַּעֲבִדוּ מִצְרַיִם אֶת־בְּנֵי יִשְׂרָאֵל בְּפָרֶךְ:
(שמות א' י"ג)

"Crushing labor" in Hebrew is *befarech*. But if read as two separate words, *befe rach*, it means "with gentle speech." The rabbis of old said that this shows how Pharaoh tricked the Israelites into working to their full strength. Pharaoh would gather them together and say, "I am going to work right along with you today; show me how well you can do. This will be a personal favor from you to me." Then he would take a shovel and a trough and begin to make bricks.

The Israelites would follow him and work unceasingly all day. At night, Pharaoh would have his captains count up the number of bricks they had made. Then he would issue an order: "I demand that the Israelites make this same number of bricks every day." (Midrash Tanḥuma, Beha'alot'chah)

"The Egyptians made the lives of the Israelites bitter with harsh labor, forcing them to build with mortar and bricks and to do all manner of field work." (Exodus 1:14) After a grueling day's work, the Israelites would be ordered to chop wood, pick vegetables from the garden, and bring water from the river for the Egyptians. (Midrash Tanḥuma, Vayeitzei)

וַיְמָרְרוּ אֶת־חַיֵּיהֶם בַּעֲבֹדָה קָשָׁה
בְּחֹמֶר וּבִלְבֵנִים וּבְכָל־עֲבֹדָה
בַּשָּׂדֶה, אֵת כָּל־עֲבֹדָתָם אֲשֶׁר־עָבְדוּ
בָהֶם בְּפָרֶךְ: (שמות א' י״ד)

In spite of Pharaoh's many cruel decrees, the Israelites continued to multiply and grow strong. Neither hard work nor humiliation could destroy them. Pharaoh became more and more frightened. In desperation, he devised a new plan, more cruel and terrible than any

וַתִּירֶאןָ הַמְיַלְּדֹת אֶת־הָאֱלֹהִים וְלֹא
עָשׂוּ כַּאֲשֶׁר דִּבֶּר אֲלֵיהֶן מֶלֶךְ
מִצְרָיִם וַתְּחַיֶּיןָ אֶת־הַיְלָדִים:
(שמות א' י"ז)

before. Pharaoh ordered the midwives Shifrah and Puah to kill all male Israelites at birth. But, fearing God, the midwives did not follow Pharaoh's command. (Exodus 1:17)

Determined to destroy the children of Israel, Pharaoh then declared, "Every son that is born shall you cast into the river and every daughter shall you keep alive." (Exodus 1:22) But our ancestors did not heed his words. When the Israelite Yocheved gave birth to a son, she placed him in a basket of reeds on the bank of the River Nile and told her daughter, Miriam, to watch over him that no harm might come to him.

One day while bathing in the Nile, Pharaoh's daughter found the basket. Her heart filled with compassion when she realized that the infant was an Israelite boy, and she adopted him. Pharaoh's daughter named the baby "Moses," which means "to pull out," and she said, "'I drew him forth from the water." (Exodus 2:10) Miriam offered to bring an Israelite woman to nurse the child, and Pharaoh's daughter agreed. Thus it was that Yocheved nursed Moses.

The story of Yocheved, Miriam, and Pharaoh's daughter models how the cause of justice and freedom can be furthered when people from diverse backgrounds—different generations, religions, and economic circumstances—work together.

Moses and Aaron before Pharaoh

HOW MOSES FREED THE ISRAELITES

Moses was raised by Pharaoh's daughter with all the luxuries of the palace. "But it came to pass, when he was grown up, that he went out among his kinfolk and witnessed their burdens." (Exodus 2:11) He responded not as a spectator, but as a kinsman. And he put his shoulder to the burden and helped every one of them.

וַיְהִי בַּיָּמִים הָהֵם וַיִּגְדַּל מֹשֶׁה וַיֵּצֵא אֶל־אֶחָיו וַיַּרְא בְּסִבְלֹתָם, וַיַּרְא אִישׁ מִצְרִי מַכֶּה אִישׁ־עִבְרִי מֵאֶחָיו:

(שמות ב׳ י״א)

Rabbi Eleazar ben Rabbi José, the Galilean, a second-century sage, taught that whenever Moses saw a child or woman carrying a crushing load, he would quickly leave his royal companions and lend his strength, pretending that it was for the sake of helping Pharaoh. That is why God said, "Since you went out of your way to see with your own eyes the suffering of Israel, and treated them as your family, I will go out of my way, and leave my place in the heavens to speak with you." (Midrash, Shemot Rabbah 1)

אָמַר הַקָּדוֹשׁ־בָּרוּךְ־הוּא, אַתָּה
הַנַּחְתָּ עֲסָקֶיךָ וְהָלַכְתָּ לִרְאוֹת
בְּצַעֲרָן שֶׁל יִשְׂרָאֵל וְנָהַגְתָּ בָּהֶן
מִנְהַג אַחִים, אֲנִי מַנִּיחַ
אֶת־הָעֶלְיוֹנִים וְאֶת־הַתַּחְתּוֹנִים
וַאֲדַבֵּר עִמָּךְ: (שמות רבא א')

One day Moses saw an Egyptian beating an Israelite. In his anger, Moses killed the Egyptian and, fearing Pharaoh, he fled to Midian. There he met Zipporah, a daughter of Jethro, the priest of Midian. They married, and Moses became shepherd to Jethro's flock.

According to an ancient legend, once, while Moses was tending Jethro's flock, God tèsted him. A kid suddenly scampered away from the flock. Moses ran after it and found it at a pool of water, where it had stopped to drink. When Moses reached the spot, he said, "I did not know it was because of thirst that you ran away. You must be weary." So he carried the kid back to the flock on his shoulders. Then God said to Moses, "Since you have shown so much kindness to a flock belonging to one of flesh and blood, you will shepherd my flock, the Israelites." (Midrash, Shemot Rabbah 2)

אָמַר הַקָּדוֹשׁ־בָּרוּךְ־הוּא יֵשׁ לְךָ
רַחֲמִים לִנְהֹג צֹאנוֹ שֶׁל בָּשָׂר־וָדָם,
כָּךְ, חַיֶּיךָ, אַתָּה תִרְעֶה צֹאנִי
יִשְׂרָאֵל: (שמות רבא ב')

"The Israelites groaned under their bondage, and they cried out....God heard their groaning and remembered the covenant." (Exodus 2:23–24) It was God's covenant with Abraham and Sarah, Isaac and Rebecca, and Jacob, Leah, and Rachel; God's covenant with the Jewish people for all time.

One day, as Moses tended his flock in the farthest corner of the wilderness, he saw a burning bush. To his amazement, the bush burned with fire but was not consumed. (Exodus 3:2) Then God called to him from the bush, saying, "Moses! Moses!"

וַיֵּרָא מַלְאַךְ יְיָ אֵלָיו
בְּלַבַּת־אֵשׁ מִתּוֹךְ הַסְּנֶה, וַיַּרְא
וְהִנֵּה הַסְּנֶה בֹּעֵר בָּאֵשׁ וְהַסְּנֶה
אֵינֶנּוּ אֻכָּל: (שמות ג׳ ב׳)

And Moses answered, *Hineini.* Here I am." (Exodus 3:4)

וַיִּקְרָא אֵלָיו אֱלֹהִים מִתּוֹךְ הַסְּנֶה
וַיֹּאמֶר מֹשֶׁה מֹשֶׁה וַיֹּאמֶר הִנֵּנִי:
(שמות ג׳ ד׳)

God said to Moses, "I am the God of your ancestors. Do not despair! Know that I am with your people, and just as this bush burns yet is not consumed, so Israel, though it suffers, will not be devoured by the Egyptians." (Midrash, Shemot Rabbah 2)

אָמַר לוֹ כְּשֵׁם שֶׁהַסְּנֶה בֹּעֵר
בָּאֵשׁ וְאֵינֶנּוּ אֻכָּל כָּךְ הַמִּצְרִים
אֵינָם יְכוֹלִים לְכַלּוֹת אֶת
יִשְׂרָאֵל: (שמות רבא ב׳)

Then God commanded Moses to return to Egypt to lead the Israelites to freedom. Armed with the promise that God had made, Moses and his brother, Aaron, presented themselves before Pharaoh and demanded that the Israelites be freed. But Pharaoh's heart was hardened, and he refused to let them go.

THE TEN PLAGUES

In sympathy for the Egyptians whose death was the price of our
freedom, we remove a drop of wine or juice from our cups by
dipping a finger in the cup and tapping it on the side of a plate
as each plague is named.

אֵלוּ עֶשֶׂר מַכּוֹת שֶׁהֵבִיא הַקָּדוֹשׁ בָּרוּךְ
הוּא עַל הַמִּצְרִים בְּמִצְרָיִם. וְאֵלוּ הֵן:
דָּם. צְפַרְדֵּעַ. כִּנִּים. עָרוֹב. דֶּבֶר. שְׁחִין.
בָּרָד. אַרְבֶּה. חֹשֶׁךְ. מַכַּת בְּכוֹרוֹת.

*Dam. Tz'fardei'a. Kinim. Arov. Dever. Sh'ḥin. Barad.
Arbeh. Ḥoshech. Makat B'chorot.*

---
29 ---

The plague
of the beasts

God brought down nine plagues upon Egypt—blood, frogs, lice, beasts, blight, boils, hail, locusts, and darkness. Yet Pharaoh remained defiant and would not let the Israelites go out from his land. But the tenth plague broke his will. As the Torah tells us, God smote every firstborn Egyptian: "From the firstborn of Pharaoh who sat on his throne, to the firstborn of the captive who was in the dungeon, and all the firstborn of the cattle. And Pharaoh arose in the night, with all his servants and all the Egyptians, for there was a great cry in Egypt; for there was no house where there was not one dead. Pharaoh summoned Moses and Aaron in the night and said, 'Rise up; go out from among my people, you and the children of Israel with you!'" (Exodus 12:29–31)

Thus were our ancestors redeemed from slavery to Pharaoh in Egypt. "Thus God took us out of Egypt with a mighty hand and an outstretched arm, with awesome power, with signs, and with wonders." (Deuteronomy 26:8)

וַיּוֹצִאֵנוּ יְיָ מִמִּצְרַיִם בְּיָד חֲזָקָה
וּבִזְרֹעַ נְטוּיָה וּבְמֹרָא גָּדֹל
וּבְאֹתוֹת וּבְמֹפְתִים: (דברים כ"ו ח)

In 1985, the Jewish communities of Israel and North America followed in God's ways and saved the Jews of Ethiopia from oppression and famine in a dramatic airlift that brought them to Israel. The mission was called "Operation Moses." Kessaye Tevajieh describes her escape at age 21.

Deciding to leave was very difficult, truly very difficult. Especially since I had to leave my parents.... But things were getting worse. Every day [in Addis Ababa] you would see people with their donkeys or on horseback. Our street was all Jews and they were all leaving. All day long and all night long too you would see people taking all their things and leaving....

I had already heard that most of the family on one side, on my mother's side...had died on the road. It was hard to hear this and to think about leaving my family. Still, in spite of all this, I finally made the decision to go.

MIRIAM'S SONG

Debbie Friedman

Based on Exodus 15:20–21

Chorus:

And the women dancing with their timbrels
Followed Miriam as she sang her song.
Sing a song to the One whom we've exalted
Miriam and the women danced and danced the whole night long.

And Miriam was a weaver of unique variety.
The tapestry she wove was one which sang our history.
With every thread and every strand she crafted her delight.
A woman touched with spirit, she dances toward the light.

And the women...

As Miriam stood upon the shores and gazed across the sea,
The wonder of this miracle she soon came to believe.
Whoever thought the sea would part with an outstretched hand,
And we should pass to freedom, and march to the promised land?

And the women...

And Miriam the Prophet took her timbrel
    in her hand,
And all the women followed her just as
    she had planned.
And Miriam raised her voice with song.
She sang with praise and might,
We've just lived through a miracle, we're
    going to dance tonight.

RIDDLE

Yocheved placed baby Moses in a basket that floated on the Nile River. What was the longest river in Egypt before the Nile was discovered?

Answer: The Nile, of course. It was there even before people discovered it!

32

A 1944 poster to raise funds for European Jews desperate to escape the Holocaust

The Passover story continues to provide a model for responding to tyranny. Under the Communist regime of the former Soviet Union, hundreds of thousands of Jews lived in poverty and oppression. The Jewish communities of Israel and North America worked in partnership to free them and bring them to safety. This poster was used to help organize the New York Jewish community's participation in Solidarity Sunday in 1979.

PHARAOH: ARCH-TYRANT

The Pharaoh we read about in the Exodus story is a tyrant who is anchored to a specific time, place, and set of events. But the Pharaoh our ancestors pictured each year, century after century, as they read the Haggadah was more than one person. Pharaoh was for them symbolic of all the cruel and heartless tyrants who had enslaved others, represented themselves as gods, or forced their wills on those they ruled.

And that is why the story of Passover is more than just the story of the emancipation the Israelites won from Pharaoh. It is the story of the emancipation the peoples of the world have won from tyrants and oppressors throughout the ages and across the globe. The first emancipation was thus only a foreshadowing of all the emancipations that were to follow and that will yet follow in the days to come. The victory over the first Pharaoh reminds us that the time will come when all the Pharaohs of the world will be vanquished, when God alone will rule over humanity, and all peoples will live in peace.

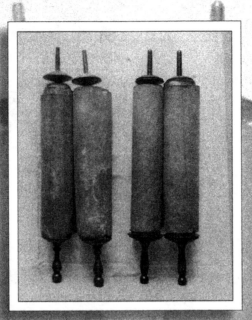

Torah scrolls brought to Savannah, Georgia, in 1733 and 1737

REMEMBER YOU WERE ONCE SLAVES!

The Israelites' suffering in Egypt, and the freedom they won, inspired many of the most beautiful teachings in the Torah. Let us now read some of them together.

אָנֹכִי יְיָ אֱלֹהֶיךָ, אֲשֶׁר הוֹצֵאתִיךָ מֵאֶרֶץ מִצְרַיִם מִבֵּית עֲבָדִים: (שמות כ׳ ב׳)

I am the Eternal One, your God, who brought you out of the land of Egypt, out of the house of bondage. (Exodus 20:2)

כִּי אֲנִי יְיָ הַמַּעֲלֶה אֶתְכֶם מֵאֶרֶץ מִצְרַיִם לִהְיֹת לָכֶם לֵאלֹהִים, וִהְיִיתֶם קְדֹשִׁים כִּי קָדוֹשׁ אָנִי: (ויקרא י״א מ״ה)

For I am the Eternal One who brought you up out of the land of Egypt, to be your God; you shall therefore be holy, for I am holy. (Leviticus 11:45)

כְּאֶזְרָח מִכֶּם יִהְיֶה לָכֶם הַגֵּר הַגָּר אִתְּכֶם
וְאָהַבְתָּ לוֹ כָּמוֹךָ, כִּי גֵרִים הֱיִיתֶם בְּאֶרֶץ
מִצְרָיִם, אֲנִי יְיָ אֱלֹהֵיכֶם: (ויקרא י״ט ל״ד)

*The stranger who sojourns with you shall be unto you
as a native among you, and you shall love the stranger
as yourself; for you were strangers in the land of Egypt:
I am the Eternal One.* (Leviticus 19:34)

וְגֵר לֹא תִלְחָץ, וְאַתֶּם יְדַעְתֶּם אֶת־נֶפֶשׁ
הַגֵּר, כִּי־גֵרִים הֱיִיתֶם בְּאֶרֶץ מִצְרָיִם:
(שמות כ״ג ט׳)

*You shall not oppress a stranger, for you know the heart
of a stranger, seeing that you were strangers in the
land of Egypt.* (Exodus 23:9)

שָׁמוֹר אֶת־יוֹם הַשַּׁבָּת לְקַדְּשׁוֹ, כַּאֲשֶׁר
צִוְּךָ יְיָ אֱלֹהֶיךָ: שֵׁשֶׁת יָמִים תַּעֲבֹד
וְעָשִׂיתָ כָּל־מְלַאכְתֶּךָ: וְיוֹם הַשְּׁבִיעִי
שַׁבָּת לַיְיָ אֱלֹהֶיךָ לֹא תַעֲשֶׂה כָל־מְלָאכָה,
אַתָּה וּבִנְךָ־וּבִתֶּךָ וְעַבְדְּךָ־וַאֲמָתֶךָ וְשׁוֹרְךָ
וַחֲמֹרְךָ וְכָל־בְּהֶמְתֶּךָ וְגֵרְךָ אֲשֶׁר
בִּשְׁעָרֶיךָ, לְמַעַן יָנוּחַ עַבְדְּךָ וַאֲמָתְךָ
כָּמוֹךָ: וְזָכַרְתָּ כִּי־עֶבֶד הָיִיתָ בְּאֶרֶץ
מִצְרַיִם וַיֹּצִאֲךָ יְיָ אֱלֹהֶיךָ מִשָּׁם בְּיָד
חֲזָקָה וּבִזְרֹעַ נְטוּיָה, עַל־כֵּן צִוְּךָ יְיָ
אֱלֹהֶיךָ לַעֲשׂוֹת אֶת־יוֹם הַשַּׁבָּת:
(דברים ה׳ י״ב-ט״ו)

35

Observe the Sabbath day, to keep it holy, as the Eternal
One your God commanded you: Six days shall you
labor, but the seventh day is the Sabbath unto the
Eternal One your God. On the seventh day you shall
not do any manner of work, neither you nor your son,
nor your daughter, nor your manservant, nor your
maidservant, nor your ox, nor your ass, nor any of
your cattle, nor your stranger who is within your gates;
that your manservant and your maidservant may rest as
well as you. And you shall remember that you were a
servant in the land of Egypt, and the Eternal One, your
God, brought you out from there by a mighty hand and
by an outstretched arm; therefore the Eternal One your
God commanded you to keep the Sabbath day.
(Deuteronomy 5:12–15)

כִּי־לִי בְנֵי־יִשְׂרָאֵל עֲבָדִים, עֲבָדַי הֵם
אֲשֶׁר־הוֹצֵאתִי אוֹתָם מֵאֶרֶץ מִצְרָיִם, אֲנִי
יְיָ אֱלֹהֵיכֶם: (ויקרא כ"ה, נ"ה)

[No Israelite shall be forever enslaved to a master], for
unto me the children of Israel are servants; they are my
servants whom I brought forth out of the land of Egypt:
I am the Eternal One your God. (Leviticus 25:55)

Tonight, at Passover
seders around the
world—even as far
away as the distant
shores of China—all
Jews are united by the
joy and traditions of the
holiday, and by the
teachings of the Torah.

DAYEINU   דַּיֵּנוּ

Fill Miriam's Cup with water. As these verses are sung, the leader raises the cup and recites each verse. The other participants sing the refrain, *Dayeinu,* which is a way of saying: For that alone, we would have been grateful.

The Cup of Miriam reminds us of the legend of Miriam's Well, which teaches that wherever our ancestors wandered in the Sinai wilderness, Miriam's Well would appear and sustain them. The Cup of Miriam symbolizes the many ways we continue to be sustained along freedom's path.

כַּמָּה מַעֲלוֹת טוֹבוֹת לַמָּקוֹם עָלֵינוּ:

Kamah ma'alot tovot lamakom aleinu:
How many wonderful deeds did God perform for us!

אִלּוּ הוֹצִיאָנוּ מִמִּצְרַיִם,
דַּיֵּנוּ:   וְלֹא קָרַע לָנוּ אֶת־הַיָּם,

Had the Compassionate One brought us out of Egypt and not split the sea for us—*Dayeinu!*

אִלּוּ קָרַע לָנוּ אֶת־הַיָּם,
דַּיֵּנוּ:   וְלֹא הֶעֱבִירָנוּ בְתוֹכוֹ בֶּחָרָבָה,

Had the Compassionate One split the Sea of Reeds for us and not brought us through dry land—*Dayeinu!*

אִלּוּ הֶעֱבִירָנוּ בְתוֹכוֹ בֶּחָרָבָה,
וְלֹא סִפֵּק צָרְכֵּנוּ בַּמִּדְבָּר
אַרְבָּעִים שָׁנָה,
דַּיֵּנוּ:

Had the Compassionate One brought us through dry
land and not sustained us in the wilderness for forty
years—*Dayeinu!*

אִלּוּ סִפֵּק צָרְכֵּנוּ בַּמִּדְבָּר
אַרְבָּעִים שָׁנָה, וְלֹא הֶאֱכִילָנוּ
אֶת־הַמָּן,
דַּיֵּנוּ:

Had the Compassionate One sustained us in the
wilderness for forty years and not fed us with
manna—*Dayeinu!*

אִלּוּ הֶאֱכִילָנוּ אֶת־הַמָּן,
וְלֹא נָתַן לָנוּ אֶת־הַשַּׁבָּת,
דַּיֵּנוּ:

Had the Compassionate One fed us with manna and
not given us Shabbat—*Dayeinu!*

אִלּוּ נָתַן לָנוּ אֶת־הַשַּׁבָּת,
וְלֹא קֵרְבָנוּ לִפְנֵי הַר סִינַי,
דַּיֵּנוּ:

Had the Compassionate One given us Shabbat and
not brought us to Mount Sinai—*Dayeinu!*

———————— 38 ————————

אִלּוּ קֵרְבָנוּ לִפְנֵי הַר סִינַי,
וְלֹא נָתַן לָנוּ אֶת־הַתּוֹרָה, דַּיֵּנוּ:

Had the Compassionate One brought us to Mount
Sinai and not given us the Torah—*Dayeinu!*

אִלּוּ נָתַן לָנוּ אֶת־הַתּוֹרָה,
וְלֹא הִכְנִיסָנוּ לְאֶרֶץ יִשְׂרָאֵל, דַּיֵּנוּ:

Had the Compassionate One given us the Torah and
not brought us into the land of Israel—*Dayeinu!*

עַל אַחַת כַּמָּה וְכַמָּה טוֹבָה כְפוּלָה
וּמְכֻפֶּלֶת לַמָּקוֹם עָלֵינוּ, שֶׁהוֹצִיאָנוּ
מִמִּצְרַיִם, וְקָרַע לָנוּ אֶת־הַיָּם, וְהֶעֱבִירָנוּ
בְתוֹכוֹ בֶּחָרָבָה, וְסִפֵּק צָרְכֵנוּ בַּמִּדְבָּר
אַרְבָּעִים שָׁנָה, וְהֶאֱכִילָנוּ אֶת־הַמָּן,
וְנָתַן לָנוּ אֶת־הַשַּׁבָּת, וְקֵרְבָנוּ לִפְנֵי הַר
סִינַי, וְנָתַן לָנוּ אֶת־הַתּוֹרָה, וְהִכְנִיסָנוּ
לְאֶרֶץ יִשְׂרָאֵל:

How much more, then, are we to be grateful to God for the
wonderful deeds that were performed for us! For the
Compassionate One brought us out of Egypt, *and* split the
Sea of Reeds for us, *and* brought us through dry land, *and*
sustained us in the wilderness for forty years, *and* fed us with
manna, *and* gave us Shabbat, *and* brought us to Mount Sinai,
and gave us the Torah, *and* brought us into the land of Israel!

פֶּסַח, מַצָּה, וּמָרוֹר

רַבָּן גַּמְלִיאֵל הָיָה אוֹמֵר, כָּל
שֶׁלֹּא אָמַר שְׁלֹשָׁה דְבָרִים אֵלּוּ
בַּפֶּסַח לֹא יָצָא יְדֵי חוֹבָתוֹ, וְאֵלּוּ
הֵן: פֶּסַח, מַצָּה, וּמָרוֹר:

The leader raises the shankbone or beet and says:

פֶּסַח שֶׁהָיוּ אֲבוֹתֵינוּ וְאִמּוֹתֵינוּ אוֹכְלִים
בִּזְמַן שֶׁבֵּית הַמִּקְדָּשׁ קַיָּם, עַל שׁוּם
מָה? עַל שׁוּם שֶׁפֶּסַח הַקָּדוֹשׁ־בָּרוּךְ־הוּא
עַל בָּתֵּי אֲבוֹתֵינוּ וְאִמּוֹתֵינוּ בְּמִצְרַיִם,
שֶׁנֶּאֱמַר, וַאֲמַרְתֶּם זֶבַח־פֶּסַח הוּא לַיָי
אֲשֶׁר פָּסַח עַל־בָּתֵּי בְנֵי־יִשְׂרָאֵל
בְּמִצְרַיִם בְּנָגְפּוֹ אֶת־מִצְרַיִם וְאֶת־
בָּתֵּינוּ הִצִּיל, וַיִּקֹּד הָעָם וַיִּשְׁתַּחֲווּ:

(שמות י״ב כ״ז)

THE THREE SYMBOLS
OF PASSOVER

Rabban Gamliel
was a Palestinian
sage who lived
at the end of the
first century and
who headed the
Academy of
Yavneh from
about 80–90 CE.

The Passover seder includes many interesting and important symbols, but three of them are so meaningful that, according to the sage Rabban Gamliel, no seder is complete unless they are fully explained. These symbols are: the *pesaḥ*, the *matzah*, and the *maror*.

The leader raises the shankbone or beet and says:

THIS BONE OF A LAMB IS THE SYMBOL OF THE PESAH LAMB. After wandering in the desert for forty years, we came to dwell in our own land where, each year, we would gather together to celebrate the Exodus from Egypt with rejoicing and festivity. Families from across the land would make the pilgrimage, and each family would bring a lamb as its special offering in honor of the festival.

This lamb was known as the *pesaḥ*, or paschal lamb, in remembrance of the time when we were spared the tragic fate of the Egyptians, whose firstborn were slain; as the Torah tells us, "God *passed over* the houses of the Israelites in Egypt when God smote the Egyptians and spared our houses." (Exodus 12:27)

*Paschal is derived
from the Greek
word for pesaḥ.*

In Hebrew, *pesaḥ* means "pass over." That is why the offering was called the *pesaḥ*, or pass-over, sacrifice; and that is why the festival is called Passover.

The leader raises the matzah and says:

מַצָּה זוּ שֶׁאָנוּ אוֹכְלִים עַל שׁוּם מָה?
עַל שׁוּם שֶׁלֹּא הִסְפִּיק בְּצֵקָם שֶׁל-
אֲבוֹתֵינוּ וְאִמּוֹתֵינוּ לְהַחֲמִיץ עַד שֶׁנִּגְלָה
עֲלֵיהֶם מֶלֶךְ מַלְכֵי הַמְּלָכִים הַקָּדוֹשׁ-
בָּרוּךְ-הוּא וּגְאָלָם, שֶׁנֶּאֱמַר, וַיֹּאפוּ
אֶת-הַבָּצֵק אֲשֶׁר הוֹצִיאוּ מִמִּצְרַיִם
עֻגֹת מַצּוֹת כִּי לֹא חָמֵץ, כִּי-גֹרְשׁוּ
מִמִּצְרַיִם וְלֹא יָכְלוּ לְהִתְמַהְמֵהַּ וְגַם-
צֵדָה לֹא-עָשׂוּ לָהֶם: (שמות י״ב ל״ט)

The leader raises the matzah and says:

THERE ARE THREE MEANINGS TO THE MATZAH.
At the beginning of our seder, we learned that the
matzah is a symbol of the bread of poverty we were
made to eat in our affliction, when we were slaves in
the land of Egypt; that it should always inspire us to
work for freedom, justice, and peace for all peoples.

The matzah reminds us, too, of the haste in which we
fled from Egypt. So hard did the Egyptians press the
Israelites that, as the Torah tells us, "They could not
tarry. So, they baked unleavened cakes of the dough
they had brought out of Egypt and did not prepare for
themselves any provision." (Exodus 12:39)

The work of redemption cannot wait. The freeing of the
oppressed, the hastening of the day when "justice shall
well up like water," cannot be delayed. (Amos 5:24) When
the moment came, we did not tarry or delay our flight to
freedom. We fled with the unleavened dough so that it
baked, unrisen, in the sun. The matzah thus reminds us
that there is no time to linger when justice waits to be done.

There is a third meaning to the matzah. In ancient
times, the Israelites lived with simplicity in the desert.
They lived in tents, dressed in plain garments, and ate
only the simplest of foods. Even their bread was only an
unleavened cake, like the matzah we eat tonight.

When the Israelites settled in Canaan, they became farm-
ers. Soon they prospered; and they began to desire more
and more material goods. Yet their desires were not sated;
instead, they grew with each new acquisition; and the
Israelites became greedy. The prophets cried out, pleading
with them to return to the modest ways of the desert.

Now the matzah has come to symbolize moderation
and balance. Let it teach us to delight not in acts of
unrestrained desire but, instead, in acts of compassion
and humanity. Luxuries can be good, adding to our
enjoyment of life. But when we live only for our
pleasure, blind to those in need, then the plea of the
prophets must be heard.

The leader raises the maror and says:

מָרוֹר שֶׁאָנוּ אוֹכְלִים עַל שׁוּם מָה?
עַל שׁוּם שֶׁמֵּרְרוּ הַמִּצְרִים אֶת־חַיֵּי
אֲבוֹתֵינוּ וְאִמּוֹתֵינוּ בְּמִצְרַיִם, שֶׁנֶּאֱמַר,
וַיְמָרְרוּ אֶת־חַיֵּיהֶם בַּעֲבֹדָה קָשָׁה
בְּחֹמֶר וּבִלְבֵנִים וּבְכָל־עֲבֹדָה בַּשָּׂדֶה,
אֶת כָּל־עֲבֹדָתָם אֲשֶׁר־עָבְדוּ בָהֶם
בְּפָרֶךְ: (שמות א' י"ד)

Clara Lemlich (shown at left, on stage, with hand raised)
personifies the qualities of urgent and determined
commitment to justice. A teenage garment worker and
activist, Lemlich attended the November 22, 1909
meeting in New York of the ladies' shirtwaist industry
workers. After hours of open debate, she stood up and,
in response to the intolerable working conditions, offered
a resolution that a strike be declared. There was wild
cheering as thousands raised their hands in agreement.
This strike came to be known as the Uprising of the
Twenty Thousand.

The leader raises the maror and says:

WE EAT THE MAROR, OR BITTER HERBS, BECAUSE OUR
OPPRESSORS EMBITTERED OUR LIVES; as the Torah tells
us, the Egyptians "made [the Israelites'] lives bitter with
hard labor in mortar and brick, and in all manner of
work in the field; all service wherein they made them
serve was with crushing labor." (Exodus 1:14)

CALL TO HALLEL

*B'chol dor vador ḥayav adam lir'ot et atzmo k'ilu hu
yatza mimitzrayim.*

In every generation, each of us should feel as though we
personally took part in the Exodus from Egypt. The Torah
tells us: "You shall tell your child on that day, saying, 'It is
because of what the Eternal One did for *me* when I came
forth out of Egypt.'" In this generation, too, we should
feel as though we, ourselves, were liberated from Egypt.

We should therefore sing praises and give thanks to the
Eternal One who did all these wonders for our ancestors
and *for us*. God brought us from slavery to freedom, and
from sorrow to joy, from mourning to festivity, from
darkness to light, and from bondage to redemption.

Let us express our gratitude and joy, let us sing a new
song before the Source of Life. Halleluyah!

Fill the second cup.

בְּכָל־דּוֹר וָדוֹר חַיָּב אָדָם לִרְאוֹת
אֶת־עַצְמוֹ כְּאִלּוּ הוּא יָצָא מִמִּצְרַיִם, שֶׁנֶּאֱמַר,
וְהִגַּדְתָּ לְבִנְךָ בַּיּוֹם הַהוּא לֵאמֹר, בַּעֲבוּר זֶה
עָשָׂה יְיָ לִי בְּצֵאתִי מִמִּצְרָיִם: (שמות י"ג ח)

לֹא אֶת־אֲבוֹתֵינוּ וְאֶת־אִמּוֹתֵינוּ בִּלְבַד גָּאַל
הַקָּדוֹשׁ־בָּרוּךְ־הוּא, אֶלָּא אַף אוֹתָנוּ גָּאַל עִמָּהֶם
שֶׁנֶּאֱמַר, וְאוֹתָנוּ הוֹצִיא מִשָּׁם, לְמַעַן הָבִיא אֹתָנוּ
לָתֶת לָנוּ אֶת־הָאָרֶץ אֲשֶׁר נִשְׁבַּע לַאֲבֹתֵינוּ:

(דברים ו' כ"ג)

לְפִיכָךְ אֲנַחְנוּ חַיָּבִים לְהוֹדוֹת, לְהַלֵּל וּלְשַׁבֵּחַ,
לְמִי שֶׁעָשָׂה לַאֲבוֹתֵינוּ וּלְאִמּוֹתֵינוּ וְלָנוּ אֶת־כָּל־
הַנִּסִּים הָאֵלּוּ. הוֹצִיאָנוּ מֵעַבְדוּת לְחֵרוּת, מִיָּגוֹן
לְשִׂמְחָה, מֵאֵבֶל לְיוֹם טוֹב, וּמֵאֲפֵלָה לְאוֹר
גָּדוֹל, וּמִשִּׁעְבּוּד לִגְאֻלָּה, וְנֹאמַר לְפָנָיו שִׁירָה
חֲדָשָׁה, הַלְלוּיָהּ:

Fill the second cup.

Abraham Joshua Heschel, a rabbi and scholar, joined
the civil rights movement because he believed that
"to care for our brother ardently, actively, is a way of
worshipping God." He is shown *(second from right)*
marching from Selma to Montgomery, Alabama, in
1965, along with *(from his right)* Ralph Bunche,
Martin Luther King, Jr., and Ralph Abernathy.

הַלֵּל

The leader alternates with the other participants in reciting the following verses:

הַלְלוּיָהּ הַלְלוּ עַבְדֵי יְיָ,
הַלְלוּ אֶת־שֵׁם יְיָ:

יְהִי שֵׁם יְיָ מְבֹרָךְ,
מֵעַתָּה וְעַד־עוֹלָם:

מִמִּזְרַח־שֶׁמֶשׁ עַד־מְבוֹאוֹ,
מְהֻלָּל שֵׁם יְיָ:

רָם עַל־כָּל־גּוֹיִם יְיָ,
עַל הַשָּׁמַיִם כְּבוֹדוֹ:

מִי כַּייָ אֱלֹהֵינוּ, הַמַּגְבִּיהִי לָשָׁבֶת:

הַמַּשְׁפִּילִי לִרְאוֹת, בַּשָּׁמַיִם וּבָאָרֶץ:

מְקִימִי מֵעָפָר דָּל,
מֵאַשְׁפֹּת יָרִים אֶבְיוֹן:

לְהוֹשִׁיבִי עִם־נְדִיבִים,
עִם נְדִיבֵי עַמּוֹ:

מוֹשִׁיבִי עֲקֶרֶת הַבַּיִת,
אֵם־הַבָּנִים שְׂמֵחָה. הַלְלוּיָהּ: (תהלים קי״ג)

48

HALLEL: PSALMS OF PRAISE

The leader alternates with the other participants in reciting the following verses:

PSALM 113

Halleluyah! Praise, O you servants of the Eternal One,
Praise the name of the Source of Life.

Praised be the name of the Source of Life,

Henceforth and forevermore!

From the rising of the sun unto the going down thereof,
Praised be the name of the Source of Life.

High above the nations is the Eternal One,

Above the heavens is God's glory.

Who is like the Eternal One, our God,
Who is enthroned on high,

Who looks down low

Upon the heavens and the earth?

Who raises up the poor out of the dust
And lifts up the needy out of the dunghill.

That God may give the needy a seat among princes,

Among the princes of God's people.

Who makes the barren woman to dwell in her house,
As a joyful mother of children. Halleluyah!

בְּצֵאת יִשְׂרָאֵל מִמִּצְרָיִם,
בֵּית יַעֲקֹב מֵעַם לֹעֵז:

הָיְתָה יְהוּדָה לְקָדְשׁוֹ,
יִשְׂרָאֵל מַמְשְׁלוֹתָיו:

הַיָּם רָאָה וַיָּנֹס, הַיַּרְדֵּן יִסֹּב לְאָחוֹר:

הֶהָרִים רָקְדוּ כְאֵילִים,
גְּבָעוֹת כִּבְנֵי־צֹאן:

מַה־לְּךָ הַיָּם כִּי תָנוּס,
הַיַּרְדֵּן תִּסֹּב לְאָחוֹר:

הֶהָרִים תִּרְקְדוּ כְאֵילִים,
גְּבָעוֹת כִּבְנֵי־צֹאן:

מִלִּפְנֵי אָדוֹן חוּלִי אָרֶץ,
מִלִּפְנֵי אֱלוֹהַּ יַעֲקֹב:

הַהֹפְכִי הַצּוּר אֲגַם־מָיִם,
חַלָּמִישׁ לְמַעְיְנוֹ־מָיִם:

(תהלים קי״ד)

PSALM 114

When Israel came forth out of Egypt,

The house of Jacob from a people of strange language,

Judah became God's sanctuary,

Israel, God's dominion.

The sea saw it and fled;

The Jordan turned backward.

The mountains skipped like rams,

The hills like young sheep.

What ails you, O sea, that you flee?

You, O Jordan, that you turn backward?

You, O mountains, that you skip like rams?

You, O hills, like young sheep?

Earth, tremble at the presence of the Eternal One,

At the presence of the God of Jacob!

Who turned the rock into a pool of water,

The flint into a fountain of waters.

We act in partnership with God to "lift up the needy" when we provide the poor and homeless with food, shelter, counseling, jobs, education, and other life-sustaining resources.

All raise the second cup and say:

בָּרוּךְ אַתָּה יְיָ אֱלֹהֵינוּ מֶלֶךְ הָעוֹלָם,
אֲשֶׁר גְּאָלָנוּ וְגָאַל אֶת אֲבוֹתֵינוּ
וְאֶת־אִמּוֹתֵינוּ מִמִּצְרַיִם, וְהִגִּיעָנוּ
לַלַּיְלָה הַזֶּה לֶאֱכָל־בּוֹ מַצָּה וּמָרוֹר:
כֵּן יְיָ אֱלֹהֵנוּ וֵאלֹהֵי אֲבוֹתֵינוּ וְאִמּוֹתֵינוּ
יַגִּיעֵנוּ לְמוֹעֲדִים וְלִרְגָלִים אֲחֵרִים
הַבָּאִים לִקְרָאתֵנוּ לְשָׁלוֹם, שְׂמֵחִים
בְּבִנְיַן אַרְצֶךְ וְשָׂשִׂים בַּעֲבוֹדָתֶךְ, וְנוֹדֶה
לְךָ שִׁיר חָדָשׁ עַל־גְּאֻלָּתֵנוּ וְעַל־פְּדוּת
נַפְשֵׁנוּ: בָּרוּךְ אַתָּה יְיָ גָּאַל יִשְׂרָאֵל:

בָּרוּךְ אַתָּה יְיָ אֱלֹהֵינוּ מֶלֶךְ הָעוֹלָם,
בּוֹרֵא פְּרִי הַגָּפֶן:

Baruch atah adonai eloheinu, melech ha'olam,
borei pri hagafen.

Drink the second cup.

All raise the second cup and say:

Praised are you, Adonai our God, Sovereign of the universe, who redeemed us and our ancestors from Egypt and enabled us to reach this night when we eat unleavened bread and bitter herbs. Thus, Eternal One our God, and God of our ancestors, may you enable us to reach other holidays and festivals (may they come to us in peace!), rejoicing in Zion rebuilt and delighting in your service. And we will thank you in new song for our redemption and deliverance. Praised are you, Eternal One, who redeems Israel.

Praised are you, Adonai our God, Sovereign of the universe, who creates the fruit of the vine.

Drink the second cup.

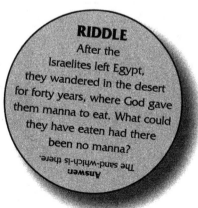

RIDDLE

After the Israelites left Egypt, they wandered in the desert for forty years, where God gave them manna to eat. What could they have eaten had there been no manna?

Answer
The sand—which is there.

B'CHOL DOR VADOR
Linda Hirschhorn

chorus: B' chol dor va-dor

b' chol dor va-dor

b' chol dor va-dor

b' chol dor va-dor   verse: In eve-ry gen - e - ra-

tion   we re-call   a time   we

fled   out   of   a   nar - row place   with

free - dom   on our   mind

(continued from page 54)

We recall how we were dancing
when we saw the waters part.
How we stood as one at Sinai
and felt the Godbeat in our heart.

B'chol dor...

Now we chant the ancient prayers
even as we sing new songs.
Link our future to the past
keep the spirit in us strong.

B'chol dor...

Sing of Miriam, sing of Deborah,
sing of Emma, sing of Szold.
In every generation
there's a story to be told.

B'chol dor...

Our rejoicing is a mixture
of the bitter and the sweet.
Until all live in freedom
our journey's not complete.

B'chol dor...

We must put an end to hunger,
hatred, crime, and war.
In every generation
that's what we're striving for.

Oh, yes, in every generation
we recall a time
we fled out of a narrow place
with freedom on our mind.

WASH HANDS רָחְצָה

All present wash their hands and recite:

בָּרוּךְ אַתָּה יְיָ אֱלֹהֵינוּ מֶלֶךְ הָעוֹלָם,
אֲשֶׁר קִדְּשָׁנוּ בְּמִצְוֹתָיו וְצִוָּנוּ עַל־
נְטִילַת יָדָיִם:

Baruch atah adonai eloheinu, melech ha'olam, asher kid'shanu b'mitzvotav v'tzivanu al n'tilat yadayim.

Praised are you, Adonai our God, Sovereign of the universe, who sanctifies us through your mitzvot and commands us to wash our hands.

MOTZI מוֹצִיא

The leader distributes portions of the upper matzah and of the remainder of the middle matzah. Then all recite together:

בָּרוּךְ אַתָּה יְיָ אֱלֹהֵינוּ מֶלֶךְ הָעוֹלָם,
הַמּוֹצִיא לֶחֶם מִן־הָאָרֶץ.

Baruch atah adonai eloheinu, melech ha'olam, hamotzi lehem min ha'aretz.

Praised are you, Adonai our God, Sovereign of the universe, who brings forth bread from the earth.

MATZAH מַצָּה

בָּרוּךְ אַתָּה יְיָ אֱלֹהֵינוּ מֶלֶךְ הָעוֹלָם, אֲשֶׁר
קִדְּשָׁנוּ בְּמִצְוֹתָיו וְצִוָּנוּ עַל־אֲכִילַת מַצָּה.

*Baruch atah adonai eloheinu, melech ha'olam, asher
kid'shanu b'mitzvotav v'tzivanu al achilat matzah.*

Praised are you, Adonai our God, Sovereign of the
universe, who sanctifies us through your mitzvot and
commands us to eat unleavened bread on Passover.

All eat the matzah.

MAROR מָרוֹר

The leader distributes the bitter herb dipped in ḥaroset. Then all
recite together:

בָּרוּךְ אַתָּה יְיָ אֱלֹהֵינוּ מֶלֶךְ הָעוֹלָם, אֲשֶׁר
קִדְּשָׁנוּ בְּמִצְוֹתָיו וְצִוָּנוּ עַל־אֲכִילַת מָרוֹר.

*Baruch atah adonai eloheinu, melech ha'olam, asher
kid'shanu b'mitzvotav v'tzivanu al achilat maror.*

Praised are you, Adonai our God, Sovereign of the
universe, who sanctifies us through your mitzvot and
commands us to eat maror on Passover.

May the sweet ḥaroset that we eat with maror remind
us of the hope of freedom that enabled our ancestors
to withstand the bitterness of their slavery.

All eat the maror dipped in ḥaroset.

Throughout the generations and across the globe, from Egypt to Israel to Babylon to Spain to Poland to the United States—in times of peace and in times of war—our people have celebrated Passover by observing the order and rituals of the seder. In this telling of a Passover spent in a Union camp during the Civil War, Joseph A. Joel describes both the festival and the follies of the night.

At dark, we had all prepared and were ready to commence the service. There being no ḥazan (cantor) present, I was selected to read the services, which I commenced by asking the blessing of the Almighty on the food before us, and to preserve our lives from danger. The ceremonies were passing off very nicely, until we arrived at the part where the bitter herb was to be taken. We all had a large portion of the herb ready to eat at the moment I said the blessing; each ate his portion, when horrors! what a scene ensued in our little congregation, it is impossible for my pen to describe.

The herb was very bitter and very fiery like cayenne pepper, and excited our thirst to such a degree that we forgot the law authorizing us to drink only four cups, and the consequence was we drank up all the cider. Those who drank the more freely became excited, and one thought he was Moses, another Aaron, and one had the audacity to call himself a pharaoh. The consequence was a skirmish, with nobody hurt—only Moses, Aaron, and Pharaoh had to be carried to the camp, and there left in the arms of Morpheus.

Approximately 10,000 Jews served in the Civil War, and over 500 died. This is a partial list of Jews wounded at the Battle of Fredericksburg. The list was published in 1862 in *The Jewish Record*, a New York City newspaper.

The verse on this Union flag is from Joshua 1:9, "Be strong and have courage; do not be terrified or dismayed, for Adonai, your God, is with you wherever you go."

Army Jews.

The following co-religionists were either killed or wounded at the battle of Fredericksburg :

T. J. Heffernam, A, 163 N. Y., hip and arm.
Serg. F. Herrfnkneckt, 7 " head.
M. Ellis, 28 N. J., hand.
Moses Steinburg, 142 Penn., legs bruised.
A. Newman, A, 72 " ankle
Lt. H. T. Davis, 81 " arm.
J. Killenback, 4 N. J., head.
S. S. Vanuess, 15 " leg.
W. Truax, 23 " back.
J. Hirsh, 4 " "
Jacob Schmidt, 19 Penn., left arm.
Jos. Osback, 19 " wounded.
W. Jabob, 19 " left arm.
Lieut. Simpson, 19 " left leg.
Capt. Schuh, 19 " wounded.
C. M. Phillips, 16 Maine, cheek.
Lieut. S. Simpson, 99 Penn., leg.
R. Harris, 107 " thigh.
L. Brauer, wounded.
—— Wolf, 5 Penn., side.
R. Ellis, 2 " leg (slight).
S. Davidson, 186 " foot.
A. Valanstein, 105 N. Y., leg.
H Stottler, 136 Penn., leg.

The above are at the hospital of Second Division, First Army Corps, in charge of Chas. J. Nordquish.

THE HILLEL SANDWICH כּוֹרֵךְ

The leader distributes a second portion of maror, which is placed between two pieces of matzah. Then all say together:

כֵּן עָשָׂה הִלֵּל בִּזְמַן שֶׁבֵּית הַמִּקְדָּשׁ קַיָּם,
הָיָה כּוֹרֵךְ (פֶּסַח) מַצָּה וּמָרוֹר וְאוֹכֵל
בְּיַחַד לְקַיֵּם מַה שֶּׁנֶּאֱמַר עַל מַצּוֹת
וּמְרֹרִים יֹאכְלֻהוּ: (במדבר ט' י"א)

Thus the sage Hillel used to do when the Temple in Jerusalem was still standing: He would place together some of the paschal lamb and some maror with matzah and eat them together, to fulfill the Biblical command: "Together with unleavened bread and bitter herbs shall they eat the paschal lamb." (Numbers 9:11)

Hillel lived in Jerusalem during the first century BCE (Before the Common Era). There he founded a school of thought known as the "House of Hillel," which was a major influence in the creation of rabbinic Judaism.

All eat the Hillel Sandwich.

THE MEAL IS SERVED שֻׁלְחָן עוֹרֵךְ

Retrieving the afikoman from its hiding place

AFIKOMAN צָפוּן

After the meal, the leader redeems the afikoman from the children and distributes a portion to each seder participant, who then eats it. It is customary to eat nothing else during the rest of the seder.

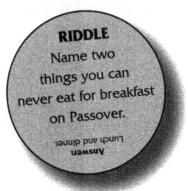

RIDDLE
Name two things you can never eat for breakfast on Passover.

Answer:
Lunch and dinner.

בָּרֵךְ

All recite together:

שִׁיר הַמַּעֲלוֹת, בְּשׁוּב יְיָ אֶת־שִׁיבַת
צִיּוֹן, הָיִינוּ כְּחֹלְמִים: אָז יִמָּלֵא שְׂחוֹק
פִּינוּ וּלְשׁוֹנֵנוּ רִנָּה, אָז יֹאמְרוּ בַגּוֹיִם,
הִגְדִּיל יְיָ לַעֲשׂוֹת עִם־אֵלֶּה:
הִגְדִּיל יְיָ לַעֲשׂוֹת עִמָּנוּ, הָיִינוּ שְׂמֵחִים:
שׁוּבָה יְיָ אֶת־שְׁבִיתֵנוּ כַּאֲפִיקִים
בַּנֶּגֶב: הַזֹּרְעִים בְּדִמְעָה, בְּרִנָּה
יִקְצֹרוּ: הָלוֹךְ יֵלֵךְ וּבָכֹה נֹשֵׂא מֶשֶׁךְ־
הַזָּרַע, בֹּא־יָבֹא בְרִנָּה נֹשֵׂא אֲלֻמֹּתָיו:

Shir hama'alot, b'shuv adonai et shivat tziyon, hayinu k'ḥolmim. Az yimalei s'ḥok pinu ulshonainu rinah, az yomru vagoyim, higdil adonai la'asot im eileh. Higdil adonai la'asot imanu, hayinu s'meiḥim. Shuvah adonai et shiviteinu ka'afikim banegev. Hazor'im b'dim'ah b'rinah yiktzoru. Haloch yeilech uvachoh nosei meshech hazara, bo yavo v'rinah nosei alumotav.

GRACE AFTER MEALS

All recite together:

PSALM 126, A SONG OF ASCENTS

When the Eternal One brought back the captives of Zion,

We were like those who dream.

Then was our mouth filled with laughter

And our tongue with singing;

They said among the nations,

"The Eternal One has done great things for these."

The Eternal One has done great things for us;

Whereupon, we rejoiced.

Turn our captivity, O Eternal One,

Like streams in the southland.

May those who sow in tears

Reap with joyous song.

May those who go on their way weeping,

Bearing the measure of seed,

Come home with joyous song,

Bearing their sheaves.

If three or more adult Jews are present, the following invitation to prayer is recited. If ten or more adult Jews are present, the reference to "eloheinu," which appears in brackets, is added.

The third cup is filled, and the leader says:

חֲבֵרַי נְבָרֵךְ:

Haveirai n'vareich.

Everyone recites, then the leader repeats:

יְהִי שֵׁם יְיָ מְבֹרָךְ מֵעַתָּה וְעַד עוֹלָם:

Y'hi sheim adonai m'vorach mei'atah v'ad olam.

Leader:

בִּרְשׁוּת חֲבֵרַי נְבָרֵךְ [אֱלֹהֵינוּ]
שֶׁאָכַלְנוּ מִשֶּׁלוֹ:

Birshut haveirai n'vareich [eloheinu] she'achalnu mishelo.

Everyone:

בָּרוּךְ [אֱלֹהֵינוּ] שֶׁאָכַלְנוּ מִשֶּׁלוֹ
וּבְטוּבוֹ חָיִינוּ:

Baruch [eloheinu] she'achalnu mishelo uvtuvo hayinu.

Leader:

בָּרוּךְ [אֱלֹהֵינוּ] שֶׁאָכַלְנוּ מִשֶּׁלוֹ
וּבְטוּבוֹ חָיִינוּ:

Baruch [eloheinu] she'achalnu mishelo uvtuvo hayinu.

Everyone:

בָּרוּךְ הוּא וּבָרוּךְ שְׁמוֹ:

Baruch hu, uvaruch sh'mo.

If three or more adult Jews are present, the following invitation to prayer is recited. If ten or more adult Jews are present, the reference to "our God," which appears in brackets, is added.

The third cup is filled, and the leader says:

We now fill our cups, for the third time, in thanksgiving for the festive meal we have just eaten. Let us say Grace.

Everyone recites, then the leader repeats:

May the name of the Eternal One be praised now and forever.

Leader:

With your permission, we praise [our God] the One whose food we have eaten.

Everyone:

Praised is [our God] the One whose food we have eaten and through whose goodness we live.

Leader:

Praised is [our God] the One whose food we have eaten and through whose goodness we live.

Everyone:

Praised be God and praised be God's name.

בָּרוּךְ אַתָּה יְיָ אֱלֹהֵינוּ מֶלֶךְ הָעוֹלָם,
הַזָּן אֶת־הָעוֹלָם כֻּלּוֹ בְּטוּבוֹ, בְּחֵן,
בְּחֶסֶד, וּבְרַחֲמִים, הוּא נוֹתֵן לֶחֶם
לְכָל־בָּשָׂר, כִּי לְעוֹלָם חַסְדּוֹ:
וּבְטוּבוֹ הַגָּדוֹל תָּמִיד לֹא־חָסַר לָנוּ,
וְאַל יֶחְסַר־לָנוּ מָזוֹן לְעוֹלָם וָעֶד,
בַּעֲבוּר שְׁמוֹ הַגָּדוֹל: כִּי הוּא אֵל
זָן וּמְפַרְנֵס לַכֹּל וּמֵטִיב לַכֹּל וּמֵכִין
מָזוֹן לְכָל־בְּרִיּוֹתָיו אֲשֶׁר בָּרָא:
בָּרוּךְ אַתָּה יְיָ, הַזָּן אֶת־הַכֹּל:

נוֹדֶה לְךָ יְיָ אֱלֹהֵינוּ עַל שֶׁהִנְחַלְתָּ
לַאֲבוֹתֵינוּ וְאִמּוֹתֵינוּ אֶרֶץ חֶמְדָּה טוֹבָה
וּרְחָבָה, וְעַל שֶׁהוֹצֵאתָנוּ יְיָ אֱלֹהֵינוּ
מֵאֶרֶץ מִצְרַיִם, וּפְדִיתָנוּ מִבֵּית עֲבָדִים,
וְעַל תּוֹרָתְךָ שֶׁלִּמַּדְתָּנוּ, וְעַל חֻקֶּיךָ
שֶׁהוֹדַעְתָּנוּ, וְעַל חַיִּים חֵן וָחֶסֶד
שֶׁחוֹנַנְתָּנוּ, וְעַל אֲכִילַת מָזוֹן שָׁאַתָּה זָן
וּמְפַרְנֵס אוֹתָנוּ תָּמִיד, בְּכָל־יוֹם
וּבְכָל־עֵת וּבְכָל־שָׁעָה:

כַּכָּתוּב, וְאָכַלְתָּ וְשָׂבָעְתָּ וּבֵרַכְתָּ אֶת־יְיָ
אֱלֹהֶיךָ עַל־הָאָרֶץ הַטֹּבָה אֲשֶׁר נָתַן־לָךְ:
בָּרוּךְ אַתָּה יְיָ עַל־הָאָרֶץ וְעַל־הַמָּזוֹן:

Praised are you, Adonai our God, Sovereign of the universe, who sustains all humankind in your goodness. Your mercy endures forever. Your great kindness protects us. May we never suffer for want of food. Praised are you, Eternal One, who provides for all your creatures.

We praise God for the land of Israel and are responsible for preserving the goodness of the land. As Jews and as citizens of a democratic country, Israelis honor the obligation and the right to work for a better society.

We give thanks to you, Adonai our God, for the gracious land, good and ample, that you gave as an inheritance to our ancestors, for that did you bring us out of the land of Egypt and deliver us from the house of bondage. We thank you for your Torah, which you have taught us, for life, and for the joy and grace in life.

The Torah commands us, "When you have eaten and are satisfied, you shall thank the Eternal One your God for the good land given to you." Praised are you, Eternal One, for the land of Israel and for sustenance.

וּבְנֵה יְרוּשָׁלַיִם עִיר הַקֹּדֶשׁ בִּמְהֵרָה
בְיָמֵינוּ: בָּרוּךְ אַתָּה יְיָ, בּוֹנֵה בְרַחֲמָיו
יְרוּשָׁלָיִם, אָמֵן:

On Shabbat add:

הָרַחֲמָן, הוּא יַנְחִילֵנוּ יוֹם שֶׁכֻּלּוֹ שַׁבָּת
וּמְנוּחָה לְחַיֵּי הָעוֹלָמִים:

הָרַחֲמָן הוּא יַנְחִילֵנוּ יוֹם שֶׁכֻּלּוֹ טוֹב:

עֹשֶׂה שָׁלוֹם בִּמְרוֹמָיו, הוּא יַעֲשֶׂה
שָׁלוֹם עָלֵינוּ, וְעַל כָּל־יִשְׂרָאֵל וְעַל
כָּל־יוֹשְׁבֵי תֵבֵל, וְאִמְרוּ, אָמֵן:

Oseh shalom bimromav, hu ya'aseh shalom aleinu, v'al
kol yisrael v'al kol yoshvei tevel, v'imru, amen.

Raise the third cup and say:

בָּרוּךְ אַתָּה יְיָ אֱלֹהֵינוּ מֶלֶךְ הָעוֹלָם,
בּוֹרֵא פְּרִי הַגָּפֶן.

Baruch atah adonai eloheinu, melech ha'olam, borei
pri hagafen.

Drink the third cup.

Rebuild Jerusalem, the holy city, soon and in our time. Praised are you, Source of Life, who in compassion renews Jerusalem. Amen.

On Shabbat add:

May you, O Merciful One, grant us a day of complete Shabbat rest, a taste of the world to come.

May you, O Merciful One, grant us a complete festival day of goodness.

May the One who makes peace in God's heavens bring peace upon all Israel and upon all the inhabitants of the earth. And let us say, Amen.

You open your hand and provide for the needs of every living thing. Happy is the one who trusts in the Creator. May God give strength to the people of Israel; may God bless them and all the creatures of the earth with peace.

Raise the third cup and say:

We are about to drink the third cup. Let us all say together:

Praised are you, Adonai our God, Sovereign of the universe, who creates the fruit of the vine.

 **Drink the third cup.**

Yad Vashem is the Holocaust Memorial located in Jerusalem. It includes a tree-lined path called the Avenue of the Righteous, which is a memorial to the non-Jews who risked their lives to save Jews.

Pour Out Your Wrath

This Haggadah introduces a new ritual. Earlier, we removed ten drops from our cup in sympathy for the Egyptians whose death was the price of our freedom. Now, as we pronounce verses of vengeance, let us remove yet another drop, to signify that anger—even justified, necessary, and righteous anger—diminishes energy that could be devoted to healing, liberation, and the repair of the world.

שְׁפֹךְ חֲמָתְךָ אֶל הַגּוֹיִם אֲשֶׁר לֹא יְדָעוּךָ
וְעַל מַמְלָכוֹת אֲשֶׁר בְּשִׁמְךָ לֹא קָרָאוּ:
כִּי אָכַל אֶת יַעֲקֹב וְאֶת נָוֵהוּ הֵשַׁמּוּ:
(תהלים ע״ט ו־ז׳)

Pour out your wrath upon the nations who do not know you,
Upon the governments who do not invoke your name.
For they have devoured Jacob
And laid waste his dwelling place. (Psalms 79:6–7)

The Holocaust did not happen in ancient times. It happened in modern times, in the middle of the 20th century. Yet, like the Pharaoh of old, the new Pharaoh was determined to annihilate the Jewish people.

Starved, humiliated, tortured though our people were, there were many acts of Jewish courage and resistance during the Holocaust. Some were heroic acts carried out, in the impulse of a terrifying moment, by an individual mother, father, grandparent, child, or neighbor. And some were sophisticated strategies implemented by the community. The largest and most famous—the Warsaw Ghetto Uprising—took place in Poland on the eve of Passover, April 19, 1943. It was the very day targeted by the Germans to deport the ghetto's inhabitants to concentration camps.

As a teenager, Mordecai Anielewicz (1919–1943) organized communal programs in the Warsaw Ghetto and other Jewish communities in Poland. The system was used to ensure, despite the Nazis, that everyone received equal rations of food and clothing, children received lessons, and newspapers were published. He formed the Jewish Fighting Organization and trained his forces to resist the Germans. On April 19, 1943, Anielewicz led the Warsaw Ghetto Uprising. He was killed three weeks later.

Pesah Has Come to the Ghetto Again

(Warsaw, April 19, 1943)

Binem Heller

Pesah has come to the Ghetto again.
The wine has no grape, the matzah no grain,
But the people anew sing the wonders of old,
The flight from the Pharaohs, so often retold.
How ancient the story, how old the refrain!

The windows are shuttered. The doors concealed.
The seder goes on. And fiction and fact
Are confused into one. Which is myth? Which is real?
"Come all who are hungry!" and children sleep, famished.
"Come all who are hungry!" and tables are bare....

Pesah has come to the Ghetto again.
The lore-laden words of the seder are said,
And the cup of the Prophet Elijah awaits,
But the Angel of Death has intruded, instead.
As always—the German snarls his commands.
As always—the words sharpened-up and precise.
As always—the fate of more Jews in his hands:
Who shall live, who shall die, this Passover night.
But no more will the Jews to the slaughter be led.
The truculent gibes of the Nazis are past.
And the lintels and doorposts tonight will be red
With the blood of free Jews who will fight to the last.

Translated from Yiddish by Max Rosenfeld

The Jews of the Warsaw Ghetto understood that their
battalion of starving civilians armed with only a few
hundred guns and homemade bombs was no match for
a modern army rich in trained soldiers, machine guns,
and tanks. Yet they fought with will and courage. It
took the Nazi troops 27 days to take the ghetto, longer
than it took them to overcome all of Poland. If the
uprising failed to liberate the Jews of Warsaw from
their oppressors, it failed with heroic glory.

THE CUP OF ELIJAH

You can fill Elijah's cup by inviting the participants to pour a bit of wine or grape juice from their cups into Elijah's. This is a reminder that redemption will come when we each have done our part to create a better world.

The leader points to the cup reserved for the Prophet Elijah and requests that the door of the house be opened to symbolize our faith in Elijah's coming. The honor of opening the door is usually given to a child. The leader then recites the following:

This is called Elijah's cup. In Jewish tradition, the Prophet Elijah is God's messenger appointed to herald the era of the Messiah, the era of peace, when the Jewish people and all peoples of the world shall be free.

Let us sing together the song of Elijah and pray that we may soon see that world of shalom.

אֵלִיָּהוּ הַנָּבִיא, אֵלִיָּהוּ הַתִּשְׁבִּי, אֵלִיָּהוּ,
אֵלִיָּהוּ, אֵלִיָּהוּ הַגִּלְעָדִי, בִּמְהֵרָה בְיָמֵינוּ
יָבֹא אֵלֵינוּ עִם־מָשִׁיחַ בֶּן־דָּוִד:

Elijah the Prophet, Elijah the Tishbite,
Elijah, Elijah, Elijah the Gileadite,
Soon, in our time, may he come, bringing with him Messiah.

The Liberty Bell in Philadelphia is inscribed with words from Leviticus 25:10: "Proclaim liberty throughout all the land unto all the inhabitants thereof."

ELIYAHU HANAVI

E - li-ya - hu ha - na - vi, e - li-ya - hu
ha - tish - bi, e - li - ya - hu, e - li - ya - hu,
e - li - ya - hu ha - gil - a - di.

FINE

Bim- hei - ra v' - ya - mei - nu ya - vo

ei - lei - nu Im ma - shi - ah ben da - vid,

im ma - shi - ah ben da - vid.

D.C. AL FINE

What can you do to help
bring about a more just and
peaceful world?

הַלֵּל

The fourth cup is poured.

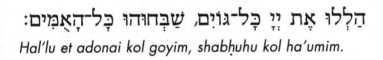

הַלְלוּ אֶת יְיָ כָּל־גּוֹיִם, שַׁבְּחוּהוּ כָּל־הָאֻמִּים:

Hal'lu et adonai kol goyim, shabḥuhu kol ha'umim.

כִּי גָבַר עָלֵינוּ חַסְדּוֹ, וֶאֱמֶת יְיָ לְעוֹלָם
הַלְלוּיָהּ:

Ki gavar aleinu ḥasdo, ve'emet adonai l'olam
hal'luyah.

הוֹדוּ לַיְיָ כִּי טוֹב	כִּי לְעוֹלָם חַסְדּוֹ:
ki l'olam ḥasdo.	Hodu ladonai ki tov
יֹאמַר־נָא יִשְׂרָאֵל	כִּי לְעוֹלָם חַסְדּוֹ:
ki l'olam ḥasdo.	Yomar na yisrael
יֹאמְרוּ־נָא בֵית־אַהֲרֹן	כִּי לְעוֹלָם חַסְדּוֹ:
ki l'olam ḥasdo.	Yomru na veit aharon
יֹאמְרוּ־נָא יִרְאֵי יְיָ	כִּי לְעוֹלָם חַסְדּוֹ:
ki l'olam ḥasdo.	Yomru na yirei adonai

HALLEL

The fourth cup is poured, and the leader says:

We fill our cups for the fourth time during this seder, before resuming the reading of the Hallel.

The leader and other participants alternate in reciting the following verses:

PSALM 117

Praise the Creator, all ye nations;

Laud God, all ye peoples!

> *For the Merciful One's lovingkindness is mighty over us,*
>
> *And the truth of God endures forever.*
>
> *Halleluyah!*

PSALM 118

Give thanks to the Creator, for God is good,

> *For God's lovingkindness endures forever.*

Let Israel now say

> *That the Creator's lovingkindness endures forever.*

Let the house of Aaron say

> *That God's lovingkindness endures forever.*

Let them that reverence the Creator say

> *That God's lovingkindness endures forever.*

מִן־הַמֵּצַר קָרָאתִי יָּה, עָנָנִי בַמֶּרְחָב יָה:
יְיָ לִי לֹא אִירָא, מַה־יַּעֲשֶׂה לִי אָדָם:...
טוֹב לַחֲסוֹת בַּיְיָ, מִבְּטֹחַ בָּאָדָם:
טוֹב לַחֲסוֹת בַּיְיָ, מִבְּטֹחַ בִּנְדִיבִים:...
דָּחֹה דְחִיתַנִי לִנְפֹּל, וַיְיָ עֲזָרָנִי:
עָזִּי וְזִמְרָת יָהּ, וַיְהִי־לִי לִישׁוּעָה:
קוֹל רִנָּה וִישׁוּעָה בְּאָהֳלֵי צַדִּיקִים,
יְמִין יְיָ עֹשָׂה חָיִל:
יְמִין יְיָ רוֹמֵמָה, יְמִין יְיָ עֹשָׂה חָיִל:
לֹא־אָמוּת כִּי־אֶחְיֶה, וַאֲסַפֵּר מַעֲשֵׂי יָהּ:
יַסֹּר יִסְּרַנִּי יָּהּ, וְלַמָּוֶת לֹא נְתָנָנִי:
פִּתְחוּ־לִי שַׁעֲרֵי־צֶדֶק, אָבֹא־בָם אוֹדֶה יָהּ:
זֶה־הַשַּׁעַר לַיְיָ, צַדִּיקִים יָבֹאוּ בוֹ:
אוֹדְךָ כִּי עֲנִיתָנִי, וַתְּהִי־לִי לִישׁוּעָה:
אֶבֶן מָאֲסוּ הַבּוֹנִים, הָיְתָה לְרֹאשׁ פִּנָּה:

מֵאֵת יְיָ הָיְתָה זֹּאת, הִיא נִפְלָאת בְּעֵינֵינוּ:
זֶה־הַיּוֹם עָשָׂה יְיָ, נָגִילָה וְנִשְׂמְחָה בוֹ:

אָנָּא יְיָ הוֹשִׁיעָה נָּא: אָנָּא יְיָ הוֹשִׁיעָה נָּא:

Ana adonai hoshi'ah na.   Ana adonai hoshi'ah na.

אָנָּא יְיָ הַצְלִיחָה נָּא: אָנָּא יְיָ הַצְלִיחָה נָּא:

Ana adonai hatzliḥah na.   Ana adonai hatzliḥah na.

(תהלים קי״ח)

From narrow straits, I called upon the Eternal One,
Who answered me with wide expanse.
> *God is for me—I will not fear;*
> *What can humankind do unto me?*
It is better to take refuge in the Eternal One
Than to trust in humankind.
> *It is better to take refuge in the Eternal One*
> *Than to trust in princes.*
I was sore beset, about to fall,
But God helped me.
> *The Eternal One is my strength and my song,*
> *And the Eternal One is my deliverance.*
The sound of joyous and triumphant song
Is in the tents of the righteous;
The right hand of the Eternal One does valiantly.
> *The right hand of the Eternal One is exalted;*
> *The right hand of the Eternal One does valiantly.*
I will not die, but live
And tell the deeds of the Eternal One.
> *God has chastened me severely*
> *But has not given me over unto death.*
Open to me the gates of victory;
I will enter into them, I will give thanks to God.
> *This is the gate of the Eternal One;*
> *The righteous shall enter into it.*
I will give thanks unto you, for you have answered me,
And have become my deliverance.
> *The stone that the builders rejected*
> *Has become the chief cornerstone.*
This is God's doing;
It is marvelous in our eyes.
> *This day God has made;*
> *We will be glad and rejoice therein.*
We beseech you, Eternal One, deliver us!
> *We beseech you, Eternal One, deliver us!*
We beseech you, Eternal One, let us prosper!
> *We beseech you, Eternal One, let us prosper!*

נִשְׁמַת כָּל־חַי תְּבָרֵךְ אֶת־שִׁמְךָ יְיָ
אֱלֹהֵינוּ, וְרוּחַ כָּל־בָּשָׂר תְּפָאֵר וּתְרוֹמֵם
זִכְרְךָ מַלְכֵּנוּ תָּמִיד: מִן־הָעוֹלָם וְעַד־הָעוֹלָם
אַתָּה אֵל, וּמִבַּלְעָדֶיךָ אֵין לָנוּ מֶלֶךְ, גּוֹאֵל
וּמוֹשִׁיעַ, פּוֹדֶה, וּמַצִּיל, וּמְפַרְנֵס, וּמְרַחֵם בְּכָל־
עֵת צָרָה וְצוּקָה, אֵין לָנוּ מֶלֶךְ אֶלָּא אָתָּה:

אִלּוּ פִינוּ מָלֵא שִׁירָה כַיָּם, וּלְשׁוֹנֵנוּ רִנָּה כַּהֲמוֹן
גַּלָּיו, וְשִׂפְתוֹתֵינוּ שֶׁבַח כְּמֶרְחֲבֵי רָקִיעַ, וְעֵינֵינוּ
מְאִירוֹת כַּשֶּׁמֶשׁ וְכַיָּרֵחַ, וְיָדֵינוּ פְרוּשׂוֹת כְּנִשְׁרֵי
שָׁמָיִם, וְרַגְלֵינוּ קַלּוֹת כָּאַיָּלוֹת, אֵין אֲנַחְנוּ
מַסְפִּיקִים לְהוֹדוֹת לְךָ יְיָ אֱלֹהֵינוּ וֵאלֹהֵי
אֲבוֹתֵינוּ וְאִמּוֹתֵינוּ, וּלְבָרֵךְ אֶת־שְׁמֶךָ,
עַל־אַחַת מֵאֶלֶף אֶלֶף אַלְפֵי אֲלָפִים וְרִבֵּי
רְבָבוֹת פְּעָמִים הַטּוֹבוֹת שֶׁעָשִׂיתָ עִם־אֲבוֹתֵינוּ
וְאִמּוֹתֵינוּ וְעִמָּנוּ:

מִמִּצְרַיִם גְּאַלְתָּנוּ יְיָ אֱלֹהֵינוּ וּמִבֵּית עֲבָדִים
פְּדִיתָנוּ, בְּרָעָב זַנְתָּנוּ וּבְשָׂבָע כִּלְכַּלְתָּנוּ,
מֵחֶרֶב הִצַּלְתָּנוּ, וּמִדֶּבֶר מִלַּטְתָּנוּ, וּמֵחֳלָיִם
רָעִים וְנֶאֱמָנִים דִּלִּיתָנוּ: עַד־הֵנָּה עֲזָרוּנוּ
רַחֲמֶיךָ וְלֹא עֲזָבוּנוּ חֲסָדֶיךָ, וְאַל תִּטְּשֵׁנוּ יְיָ
אֱלֹהֵינוּ לָנֶצַח:

Conclusion of the Hallel

The breath of all that lives shall acclaim your name, Eternal One our God, and the spirit of all creatures shall ever glorify and exalt you, O our Sovereign. From everlasting unto everlasting, you are God, and besides you we have no sovereign who redeems and delivers and sustains, and who in all times of trouble and stress shows compassion. Truly we have no sovereign but you.

Though our mouths were as filled with song as the sea, and our tongues with joy as the multitude of its waves, and our lips with praise as the wide expanse of the firmament; though our eyes were radiant as the sun and the moon, and our hands were spread forth like the eagles of heaven, and our feet were swift as hinds, yet should we be unequal to thanking you, Eternal One our God, and God of our ancestors, for one small measure of the kindness you have shown to our ancestors and to us.

From Egypt, you redeemed us, Eternal One our God, and from the house of bondage, you delivered us. In famine, you fed us and in plenty, sustained us. From the sword, you rescued us and from pestilence, saved us; from sore and grievous ills, you protected us. Ever have your tender mercies helped us; and your lovingkindness has not deserted us. May you never forsake us, Eternal One our God.

Given that the founding fathers of the United States of America were well-versed in biblical texts and were particularly identified with the liberation story of Exodus, it is interesting that the bald eagle was adopted as the national bird of the United States in 1782. The symbol conjures up God's declaration: "You have seen what I did to Egypt and how I bore you on eagles' wings and brought you to myself." (Exodus 19:4)

כִּי לוֹ נָאֶה

<table>
<tr><td>

2

דָּגוּל בִּמְלוּכָה
הָדוּר כַּהֲלָכָה
וָתִיקָיו יֹאמְרוּ לוֹ
לְךָ וּלְךָ
לְךָ כִּי לְךָ
לְךָ אַף לְךָ
לְךָ יְיָ הַמַּמְלָכָה
כִּי לוֹ נָאֶה כִּי לוֹ יָאֶה:

</td><td>

1

אַדִּיר בִּמְלוּכָה
בָּחוּר כַּהֲלָכָה
גְּדוּדָיו יֹאמְרוּ לוֹ
לְךָ וּלְךָ
לְךָ כִּי לְךָ
לְךָ אַף לְךָ
לְךָ יְיָ הַמַּמְלָכָה
כִּי לוֹ נָאֶה כִּי לוֹ יָאֶה:

</td></tr>
<tr><td>

4

יָחִיד בִּמְלוּכָה
כַּבִּיר כַּהֲלָכָה
לִמּוּדָיו יֹאמְרוּ לוֹ
לְךָ וּלְךָ
לְךָ כִּי לְךָ
לְךָ אַף לְךָ
לְךָ יְיָ הַמַּמְלָכָה
כִּי לוֹ נָאֶה כִּי לוֹ יָאֶה:

</td><td>

3

זַכַּאי בִּמְלוּכָה
חָסִין כַּהֲלָכָה
טַפְסְרָיו יֹאמְרוּ לוֹ
לְךָ וּלְךָ
לְךָ כִּי לְךָ
לְךָ אַף לְךָ
לְךָ יְיָ הַמַּמְלָכָה
כִּי לוֹ נָאֶה כִּי לוֹ יָאֶה:

</td></tr>
<tr><td>

6

עָנָיו בִּמְלוּכָה
פּוֹדֶה כַּהֲלָכָה
צַדִּיקָיו יֹאמְרוּ לוֹ
לְךָ וּלְךָ
לְךָ כִּי לְךָ
לְךָ אַף לְךָ
לְךָ יְיָ הַמַּמְלָכָה
כִּי לוֹ נָאֶה כִּי לוֹ יָאֶה:

</td><td>

5

מוֹשֵׁל בִּמְלוּכָה
נוֹרָא כַּהֲלָכָה
סְבִיבָיו יֹאמְרוּ לוֹ
לְךָ וּלְךָ
לְךָ כִּי לְךָ
לְךָ אַף לְךָ
לְךָ יְיָ הַמַּמְלָכָה
כִּי לוֹ נָאֶה כִּי לוֹ יָאֶה:

</td></tr>
</table>

קָדוֹשׁ בִּמְלוּכָה   תַּקִּיף בִּמְלוּכָה

רַחוּם כַּהֲלָכָה   תּוֹמֵךְ כַּהֲלָכָה

שִׁנְאַנָּיו יֹאמְרוּ לוֹ   תְּמִימָיו יֹאמְרוּ לוֹ

לְךָ וּלְךָ   לְךָ וּלְךָ

לְךָ כִּי לְךָ   לְךָ כִּי לְךָ

לְךָ אַף לְךָ   לְךָ אַף לְךָ

לְךָ יְיָ הַמַּמְלָכָה   לְךָ יְיָ הַמַּמְלָכָה

כִּי לוֹ נָאֶה כִּי לוֹ יָאֶה: כִּי לוֹ נָאֶה כִּי לוֹ יָאֶה:

TO YOU PRAISE IS DUE

Glorious in sovereignty;
Worthily adored,
Your hosts all say to you,
To you, Eternal One, say to you,
To you, yes, to you,
Yours, O God, is sovereignty,
To you praise belongs, to you praise is due.

> The additional Hebrew stanzas substitute synonyms for the words *glorious*, *adored* and *your hosts* and conclude with the refrain "To you, Eternal One, . . . "

אַדִּיר הוּא

בָּחוּר הוּא
גָּדוֹל הוּא
דָּגוּל הוּא
הָדוּר הוּא
יִבְנֶה בֵיתוֹ בְּקָרוֹב
בִּמְהֵרָה, בִּמְהֵרָה,
בְּיָמֵינוּ, בְּקָרוֹב,
אֵל בְּנֵה, אֵל בְּנֵה,
בְּנֵה בֵיתְךָ בְּקָרוֹב:

אַדִּיר הוּא
אַדִּיר הוּא
יִבְנֶה בֵיתוֹ בְּקָרוֹב
בִּמְהֵרָה, בִּמְהֵרָה,
בְּיָמֵינוּ, בְּקָרוֹב
אֵל בְּנֵה, אֵל בְּנֵה,
בְּנֵה בֵיתְךָ בְּקָרוֹב:

יָחִיד הוּא
כַּבִּיר הוּא
לָמוּד הוּא
מֶלֶךְ הוּא
יִבְנֶה בֵיתוֹ בְּקָרוֹב
בִּמְהֵרָה, בִּמְהֵרָה,
בְּיָמֵינוּ, בְּקָרוֹב,
אֵל בְּנֵה, אֵל בְּנֵה,
בְּנֵה בֵיתְךָ בְּקָרוֹב:

וָתִיק הוּא
זַכַּאי הוּא
חָסִיד הוּא
טָהוֹר הוּא
יִבְנֶה בֵיתוֹ בְּקָרוֹב
בִּמְהֵרָה, בִּמְהֵרָה,
בְּיָמֵינוּ, בְּקָרוֹב,
אֵל בְּנֵה, אֵל בְּנֵה,
בְּנֵה בֵיתְךָ בְּקָרוֹב:

The word *Temple* is to be understood here figuratively as referring to the land of Israel as the religious center of the Jewish people.

6	5
צַדִּיק הוּא	נָאוֹר הוּא
קָדוֹשׁ הוּא	שַׂגִּיב הוּא
רַחוּם הוּא	עִזּוּז הוּא
שַׁדַּי הוּא	פּוֹדֶה הוּא
תַּקִּיף הוּא	יִבְנֶה בֵיתוֹ בְּקָרוֹב
יִבְנֶה בֵיתוֹ בְּקָרוֹב	בִּמְהֵרָה, בִּמְהֵרָה,
בִּמְהֵרָה, בִּמְהֵרָה,	בְּיָמֵינוּ, בְּקָרוֹב,
בְּיָמֵינוּ, בְּקָרוֹב	אֵל בְּנֵה, אֵל בְּנֵה,
אֵל בְּנֵה, אֵל בְּנֵה,	בְּנֵה בֵיתְךָ בְּקָרוֹב:
בְּנֵה בֵיתְךָ בְּקָרוֹב:	

GLORIOUS IS GOD

Glorious is God,
Glorious is God.
God will rebuild the Holy Temple
Speedily, speedily,
In our days and soon,
Build it, Eternal One! Build it, Eternal One!

The additional Hebrew stanzas substitute synonyms for *glorious* and conclude
with the refrain "God will rebuild the Holy Temple . . ."

EHAD MI YODEI'A

Lightly, gaily   Traditional

E - ḥad mi yo - dei' - a? E - ḥad a - ni yo -

dei' - a. E - ḥad —— e - lo - hei - nu she - ba - sha -

ma - yim u - va' - a - retz.   Shna - yim mi - yo -

אֶחָד מִי יוֹדֵעַ

אֶחָד מִי יוֹדֵעַ?
אֶחָד אֲנִי יוֹדֵעַ. אֶחָד אֱלֹהֵינוּ שֶׁבַּשָּׁמַיִם
וּבָאָרֶץ.

שְׁנַיִם מִי יוֹדֵעַ?
שְׁנַיִם אֲנִי יוֹדֵעַ. שְׁנֵי לֻחוֹת הַבְּרִית. אֶחָד
אֱלֹהֵינוּ שֶׁבַּשָּׁמַיִם וּבָאָרֶץ.

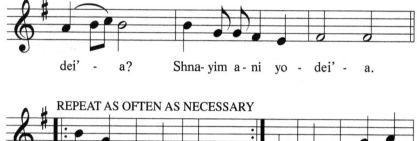

dei' - a? Shna- yim a - ni yo - dei' - a.

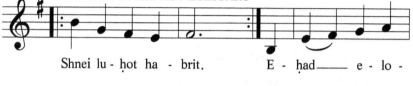

REPEAT AS OFTEN AS NECESSARY

Shnei lu - ḥot ha - brit. E - ḥad— e - lo -

hei - nu she - ba - sha - ma - yim u - va' - a - retz.

WHO KNOWS ONE?

The leader reads the questions, and the other participants recite the answer:

I'll tell you a number, and you must say
The meaning it has for us today.
The number one I have in mind;
My meaning what wise child can find?

> *I know the meaning of number one;*
> *One stands for the Eternal One our God alone.*

Who knows the meaning of number two?
If you know the answer, tell me true.

> *Two stands for the tablets made of stone,*
> *With the Ten Commandments writ thereon.*
> *One stands for the Eternal One our God alone.*

שְׁלֹשָׁה מִי יוֹדֵעַ?

שְׁלֹשָׁה אֲנִי יוֹדֵעַ. שְׁלֹשָׁה אָבוֹת. שְׁנֵי לֻחוֹת הַבְּרִית. אֶחָד אֱלֹהֵינוּ שֶׁבַּשָּׁמַיִם וּבָאָרֶץ.

אַרְבַּע מִי יוֹדֵעַ?

אַרְבַּע אֲנִי יוֹדֵעַ. אַרְבַּע אִמָּהוֹת. שְׁלֹשָׁה אָבוֹת. שְׁנֵי לֻחוֹת הַבְּרִית. אֶחָד אֱלֹהֵינוּ שֶׁבַּשָּׁמַיִם וּבָאָרֶץ.

חֲמִשָּׁה מִי יוֹדֵעַ?

חֲמִשָּׁה אֲנִי יוֹדֵעַ. חֲמִשָּׁה חֻמְשֵׁי תוֹרָה. אַרְבַּע אִמָּהוֹת. שְׁלֹשָׁה אָבוֹת. שְׁנֵי לֻחוֹת הַבְּרִית. אֶחָד אֱלֹהֵינוּ שֶׁבַּשָּׁמַיִם וּבָאָרֶץ.

שִׁשָּׁה מִי יוֹדֵעַ?

שִׁשָּׁה אֲנִי יוֹדֵעַ. שִׁשָּׁה סִדְרֵי מִשְׁנָה. חֲמִשָּׁה חֻמְשֵׁי תוֹרָה. אַרְבַּע אִמָּהוֹת. שְׁלֹשָׁה אָבוֹת. שְׁנֵי לֻחוֹת הַבְּרִית. אֶחָד אֱלֹהֵינוּ שֶׁבַּשָּׁמַיִם וּבָאָרֶץ.

Who knows the meaning of number three?
If you know the answer, tell it to me.

> *Three stands for the fathers of our line*
> *On whom God showered love divine.*
> *Two stands for the tablets made of stone;*
> *One stands for the Eternal One our God alone.*

Who knows the meaning of number four?
If you answer that, I'll ask some more.

> *Four stands for the mothers of grace sublime*
> *On them God showered love divine.*
> *Three stands for the fathers of our line;*
> *Two stands for the tablets made of stone;*
> *One stands for the Eternal One our God alone.*

Who knows the meaning of number five?
What it means has kept our people alive.

> *Five stands for the five books of Torah*
> *Which Jews study with love and awe.*
> *Four stands for the mothers of grace sublime;*
> *Three stands for the fathers of our line;*
> *Two stands for the tablets made of stone;*
> *One stands for the Eternal One our God alone.*

Who knows the meaning of number six?
A fact well learned in the memory sticks.

> *Six stands for the six books of Mishnah*
> *In which is preserved the Oral Law.*
> *Five stands for the five books of Torah;*
> *Four stands for the mothers of grace sublime;*
> *Three stands for the fathers of our line;*
> *Two stands for the tablets made of stone;*
> *One stands for the Eternal One our God alone.*

שִׁבְעָה מִי יוֹדֵעַ?

שִׁבְעָה אֲנִי יוֹדֵעַ. שִׁבְעָה יְמֵי שַׁבְּתָא. שִׁשָּׁה
סִדְרֵי מִשְׁנָה. חֲמִשָּׁה חֻמְשֵׁי תוֹרָה. אַרְבַּע
אִמָּהוֹת. שְׁלֹשָׁה אָבוֹת. שְׁנֵי לֻחוֹת הַבְּרִית.
אֶחָד אֱלֹהֵינוּ שֶׁבַּשָּׁמַיִם וּבָאָרֶץ.

שְׁמוֹנָה מִי יוֹדֵעַ?

שְׁמוֹנָה אֲנִי יוֹדֵעַ. שְׁמוֹנָה יְמֵי מִילָה. שִׁבְעָה
יְמֵי שַׁבְּתָא. שִׁשָּׁה סִדְרֵי מִשְׁנָה. חֲמִשָּׁה
חֻמְשֵׁי תוֹרָה. אַרְבַּע אִמָּהוֹת. שְׁלֹשָׁה
אָבוֹת. שְׁנֵי לֻחוֹת הַבְּרִית. אֶחָד אֱלֹהֵינוּ
שֶׁבַּשָּׁמַיִם וּבָאָרֶץ.

תִּשְׁעָה מִי יוֹדֵעַ?

תִּשְׁעָה אֲנִי יוֹדֵעַ. תִּשְׁעָה יַרְחֵי לֵדָה.
שְׁמוֹנָה יְמֵי מִילָה. שִׁבְעָה יְמֵי שַׁבְּתָא. שִׁשָּׁה
סִדְרֵי מִשְׁנָה. חֲמִשָּׁה חֻמְשֵׁי תוֹרָה. אַרְבַּע
אִמָּהוֹת. שְׁלֹשָׁה אָבוֹת. שְׁנֵי לֻחוֹת הַבְּרִית.
אֶחָד אֱלֹהֵינוּ שֶׁבַּשָּׁמַיִם וּבָאָרֶץ.

Who knows the meaning of number seven?
In our Bible's first story the meaning is given.

> *Seven is the count for the Sabbath day*
> *That ends the week with prayer and praise.*
> *Six stands for the six books of Mishnah;*
> *Five stands for the five books of Torah;*
> *Four stands for the mothers of grace sublime;*
> *Three stands for the fathers of our line;*
> *Two stands for the tablets made of stone;*
> *One stands for the Eternal One our God alone.*

Who knows the meaning of number eight?
Answer promptly; don't make us wait.

> *Eight stands for an infant's waiting days*
> *And the covenant entered with feast and praise.*
> *Seven is the count for the Sabbath day;*
> *Six stands for the six books of Mishnah;*
> *Five stands for the five books of Torah;*
> *Four stands for the mothers of grace sublime;*
> *Three stands for the fathers of our line;*
> *Two stands for the tablets made of stone;*
> *One stands for the Eternal One our God alone.*

Who knows the meaning of number nine?
If you know the answer, just give a sign.

> *Nine stands for the months awaiting cheer*
> *As each new birth brings redemption near.*
> *Eight stands for an infant's waiting days;*
> *Seven is the count for the Sabbath day;*
> *Six stands for the six books of Mishnah;*
> *Five stands for the five books of Torah;*
> *Four stands for the mothers of grace sublime;*
> *Three stands for the fathers of our line;*
> *Two stands for the tablets made of stone;*
> *One stands for the Eternal One our God alone.*

עֲשָׂרָה מִי יוֹדֵעַ?

עֲשָׂרָה אֲנִי יוֹדֵעַ. עֲשָׂרָה דִבְּרַיָּא. תִּשְׁעָה
יַרְחֵי לֵדָה. שְׁמוֹנָה יְמֵי מִילָה. שִׁבְעָה יְמֵי
שַׁבְּתָא. שִׁשָּׁה סִדְרֵי מִשְׁנָה. חֲמִשָּׁה חֻמְשֵׁי
תוֹרָה. אַרְבַּע אִמָּהוֹת. שְׁלשָׁה אָבוֹת. שְׁנֵי
לֻחוֹת הַבְּרִית. אֶחָד אֱלֹהֵינוּ שֶׁבַּשָּׁמַיִם
וּבָאָרֶץ.

אַחַד עָשָׂר מִי יוֹדֵעַ?

אַחַד עָשָׂר אֲנִי יוֹדֵעַ. אַחַד עָשָׂר כּוֹכְבַיָּא.
עֲשָׂרָה דִבְּרַיָּא. תִּשְׁעָה יַרְחֵי לֵדָה. שְׁמוֹנָה
יְמֵי מִילָה. שִׁבְעָה יְמֵי שַׁבְּתָא. שִׁשָּׁה סִדְרֵי
מִשְׁנָה. חֲמִשָּׁה חֻמְשֵׁי תוֹרָה. אַרְבַּע אִמָּהוֹת.
שְׁלשָׁה אָבוֹת. שְׁנֵי לֻחוֹת הַבְּרִית. אֶחָד
אֱלֹהֵינוּ שֶׁבַּשָּׁמַיִם וּבָאָרֶץ.

שְׁנֵים עָשָׂר מִי יוֹדֵעַ?

שְׁנֵים עָשָׂר אֲנִי יוֹדֵעַ. שְׁנֵים עָשָׂר שִׁבְטַיָּא.
אַחַד עָשָׂר כּוֹכְבַיָּא. עֲשָׂרָה דִבְּרַיָּא.
תִּשְׁעָה יַרְחֵי לֵדָה. שְׁמוֹנָה יְמֵי מִילָה.

Who knows the meaning of number ten?
Children who know grow up strong women and men.

> Ten stands for the Ten Commandments clear
> Received by our ancestors with love and fear.
> Nine stands for the months awaiting cheer;
> Eight stands for an infant's waiting days;
> Seven is the count for the Sabbath day;
> Six stands for the six books of Mishnah;
> Five stands for the five books of Torah;
> Four stands for the mothers of grace sublime;
> Three stands for the fathers of our line;
> Two stands for the tablets made of stone;
> One stands for the Eternal One our God alone.

Who knows the meaning of number eleven?
If you want a hint, look toward heaven.

> Eleven stands for the stars that did seem
> To bow to Joseph in his dream.
> Ten stands for the Ten Commandments clear;
> Nine stands for the months awaiting cheer;
> Eight stands for an infant's waiting days;
> Seven is the count for the Sabbath day;
> Six stands for the six books of Mishnah;
> Five stands for the five books of Torah;
> Four stands for the mothers of grace sublime;
> Three stands for the fathers of our line;
> Two stands for the tablets made of stone;
> One stands for the Eternal One our God alone.

Who knows the meaning of number twelve?
Into your knowledge of history delve.

> Twelve tribes from Egypt did God redeem;
> Their redemption is this festival's theme.
> Eleven the stars of Joseph's dream;
> Ten stands for the Ten Commandments clear;

שִׁבְעָה יְמֵי שַׁבְּתָא. שִׁשָּׁה סִדְרֵי מִשְׁנָה.
חֲמִשָּׁה חֻמְשֵׁי תוֹרָה. אַרְבַּע אִמָּהוֹת.
שְׁלֹשָׁה אָבוֹת. שְׁנֵי לֻחוֹת הַבְּרִית. אֶחָד
אֱלֹהֵינוּ שֶׁבַּשָּׁמַיִם וּבָאָרֶץ.

שְׁלֹשָׁה עָשָׂר מִי יוֹדֵעַ?
שְׁלֹשָׁה עָשָׂר אֲנִי יוֹדֵעַ. שְׁלֹשָׁה
עָשָׂר מִדַּיָּא. שְׁנֵים עָשָׂר שִׁבְטַיָּא.
אַחַד עָשָׂר כּוֹכְבַיָּא. עֲשָׂרָה דִבְּרַיָּא.
תִּשְׁעָה יַרְחֵי לֵדָה. שְׁמוֹנָה יְמֵי מִילָה.
שִׁבְעָה יְמֵי שַׁבְּתָא. שִׁשָּׁה סִדְרֵי מִשְׁנָה.
חֲמִשָּׁה חֻמְשֵׁי תוֹרָה. אַרְבַּע אִמָּהוֹת.
שְׁלֹשָׁה אָבוֹת. שְׁנֵי לֻחוֹת הַבְּרִית. אֶחָד
אֱלֹהֵינוּ שֶׁבַּשָּׁמַיִם וּבָאָרֶץ.

There are many
camels in Israel.
When you visit, you
can ride on one.

Nine stands for the months awaiting cheer;
Eight stands for an infant's waiting days;
Seven is the count for the Sabbath day;
Six stands for the six books of Mishnah;
Five stands for the five books of Torah;
Four stands for the mothers of grace sublime;
Three stands for the fathers of our line;
Two stands for the tablets made of stone;
One stands for the Eternal One our God alone.

Who knows the meaning of number thirteen?
It will be clear to those whose minds are keen.

Thirteen are the attributes of God
Twelve stands for the tribes God did redeem;
Eleven stands for the stars of Joseph's dream;
Ten stands for the Ten Commandments clear;
Nine stands for the months awaiting cheer;
Eight stands for an infant's waiting days;
Seven is the count for the Sabbath day;
Six stands for the six books of Mishnah;
Five stands for the five books of Torah;
Four stands for the mothers of grace sublime;
Three stands for the fathers of our line;
Two stands for the tablets made of stone;
One stands for the Eternal One our God alone.

RIDDLE
How do you get down from a camel?

Answer
You don't get down from a camel. You get down from a duck.

HAD GADYA   חַד גַּדְיָא

Although this Aramaic folk song speaks of a goat, a cat, a dog, and many other things, symbolically, it tells the story of the Jewish people's history. It refers to how Israel was first conquered by Babylonia, how Babylonia was then destroyed by Persia, how the Persians in turn were defeated by the Macedonians, and they by the Romans, and so on.

To keep the interest of the children, some families assign parts, with individual participants making the sounds of the kid, cat, dog, etc.

HAD GADYA

Gaily   Traditional

Had gad - ya——— had gad - ya. Di - z' - van a - ba

bi - trei zu - zei had gad - ya——— had gad - ya.

Va' - a - ta shun - ra v' - a - chal l'-gad - ya di -

z' - van a - ba bi - trei zu - zei had gad - ya———

had gad - ya.

"Ḥad Gadya" closes with the hope that someday God will put an end to all those who do evil and will rebuild the world so that peace can flourish. Through acts of justice and mercy, we, our children, and our children's children become God's outstretched arm and help turn this hope into reality.

An only kid! An only kid!	חַד גַּדְיָא חַד גַּדְיָא
My father bought for two *zuzim*.	דְּזַבֵּן אַבָּא בִּתְרֵי זוּזֵי
An only kid! An only kid!	חַד גַּדְיָא חַד גַּדְיָא:
Then came the cat	וְאָתָא שׁוּנְרָא
And ate the kid	וְאָכַל לְגַדְיָא
My father bought for two *zuzim*.	דְּזַבֵּן אַבָּא בִּתְרֵי זוּזֵי
An only kid! An only kid!	חַד גַּדְיָא חַד גַּדְיָא:
Then came the dog	וְאָתָא כַלְבָּא
And bit the cat,	וְנָשַׁךְ לְשׁוּנְרָא
That ate the kid	דְּאָכַל לְגַדְיָא
My father bought for two *zuzim*.	דְּזַבֵּן אַבָּא בִּתְרֵי זוּזֵי
An only kid! An only kid!	חַד גַּדְיָא חַד גַּדְיָא:
Then came the stick	וְאָתָא חוּטְרָא
And beat the dog	וְהִכָּה לְכַלְבָּא
That bit the cat,	דְּנָשַׁךְ לְשׁוּנְרָא
That ate the kid	דְּאָכַל לְגַדְיָא
My father bought for two *zuzim*.	דְּזַבֵּן אַבָּא בִּתְרֵי זוּזֵי
An only kid! An only kid!	חַד גַּדְיָא חַד גַּדְיָא:
Then came the fire	וְאָתָא נוּרָא
And burned the stick,	וְשָׂרַף לְחוּטְרָא
That beat the dog,	דְּהִכָּה לְכַלְבָּא
That bit the cat,	דְּנָשַׁךְ לְשׁוּנְרָא
That ate the kid	דְּאָכַל לְגַדְיָא
My father bought for two *zuzim*.	דְּזַבֵּן אַבָּא בִּתְרֵי זוּזֵי
An only kid! An only kid!	חַד גַּדְיָא חַד גַּדְיָא:

Then came the water	וְאָתָא מַיָּא
And quenched the fire,	וְכָבָה לְנוּרָא
That burned the stick,	דְּשָׂרַף לְחוּטְרָא
That beat the dog,	דְּהִכָּה לְכַלְבָּא
That bit the cat,	דְּנָשַׁךְ לְשׁוּנְרָא
That ate the kid	דְּאָכַל לְגַדְיָא
My father bought for two *zuzim*.	דְּזַבֵּן אַבָּא בִּתְרֵי זוּזֵי
An only kid! An only kid!	חַד גַּדְיָא חַד גַּדְיָא:

Then came the ox	וְאָתָא תוֹרָא
And drank the water,	וְשָׁתָא לְמַיָּא
That quenched the fire,	דְּכָבָה לְנוּרָא
That burned the stick,	דְּשָׂרַף לְחוּטְרָא
That beat the dog,	דְּהִכָּה לְכַלְבָּא
That bit the cat,	דְּנָשַׁךְ לְשׁוּנְרָא
That ate the kid	דְּאָכַל לְגַדְיָא
My father bought for two *zuzim*.	דְּזַבֵּן אַבָּא בִּתְרֵי זוּזֵי
An only kid! An only kid!	חַד גַּדְיָא חַד גַּדְיָא:

Then came the *shoḥeit*	וְאָתָא הַשּׁוֹחֵט
And slaughtered the ox,	וְשָׁחַט לְתוֹרָא
That drank the water,	דְּשָׁתָא לְמַיָּא
That quenched the fire,	דְּכָבָה לְנוּרָא
That burned the stick,	דְּשָׂרַף לְחוּטְרָא
That beat the dog,	דְּהִכָּה לְכַלְבָּא
That bit the cat,	דְּנָשַׁךְ לְשׁוּנְרָא
That ate the kid	דְּאָכַל לְגַדְיָא
My father bought for two *zuzim*.	דְּזַבֵּן אַבָּא בִּתְרֵי זוּזֵי
An only kid! An only kid!	חַד גַּדְיָא חַד גַּדְיָא:

Then came the angel of death	וְאָתָא מַלְאַךְ הַמָּוֶת
And slew the *shoḥeit*,	וְשָׁחַט לְשׁוֹחֵט
That slaughtered the ox,	דְּשָׁחַט לְתוֹרָא
That drank the water,	דְּשָׁתָא לְמַיָּא
That quenched the fire,	דְּכָבָה לְנוּרָא
That burned the stick,	דְּשָׂרַף לְחוּטְרָא
That beat the dog,	דְּהִכָּה לְכַלְבָּא
That bit the cat,	דְּנָשַׁךְ לְשׁוּנְרָא
That ate the kid	דְּאָכַל לְגַדְיָא
My father bought for two *zuzim*.	דְּזַבִּן אַבָּא בִּתְרֵי זוּזֵי
An only kid! An only kid!	חַד גַּדְיָא חַד גַּדְיָא:

Then came the Holy One,	וְאָתָא הַקָּדוֹשׁ
praised be God,	בָּרוּךְ הוּא
And destroyed the angel of death,	וְשָׁחַט לְמַלְאַךְ הַמָּוֶת
That slew the *shoḥeit*,	דְּשָׁחַט לְשׁוֹחֵט
That slaughtered the ox,	דְּשָׁחַט לְתוֹרָא
That drank the water,	דְּשָׁתָא לְמַיָּא
That quenched the fire,	דְּכָבָה לְנוּרָא
That burned the stick,	דְּשָׂרַף לְחוּטְרָא
That beat the dog,	דְּהִכָּה לְכַלְבָּא
That bit the cat,	דְּנָשַׁךְ לְשׁוּנְרָא
That ate the kid	דְּאָכַל לְגַדְיָא
My father bought for two *zuzim*.	דְּזַבִּן אַבָּא בִּתְרֵי זוּזֵי
An only kid! An only kid!	חַד גַּדְיָא חַד גַּדְיָא:

A *shoḥeit* is one who is trained in the laws of the kosher slaughtering of animals.

Lo Yisa Goy   לֹא יִשָּׂא גוֹי

This Passover night, let us sing out the Prophet Isaiah's vision of a world that is free of violence and war. (Isaiah 2:4) And let us work in community with others to transform that vision into a reality.

לֹא יִשָּׂא גוֹי אֶל גוֹי חֶרֶב,
לֹא יִלְמְדוּ עוֹד מִלְחָמָה:

Lo yisa goy el goy herev, lo yilm'du od milhamah.

Nation shall not lift up sword against nation, neither shall they study war anymore.

Raise the fourth cup and say:

בָּרוּךְ אַתָּה יְיָ אֱלֹהֵינוּ מֶלֶךְ
הָעוֹלָם, בּוֹרֵא פְּרִי הַגָּפֶן.

Baruch atah adonai eloheinu, melech ha'olam, borei pri hagafen.

Praised are you, Adonai our God, Sovereign of the universe, who creates the fruit of the vine.

 **Drink the fourth cup.**

חֲסַל סִדּוּר פֶּסַח כְּהִלְכָתוֹ,
כְּכָל מִשְׁפָּטוֹ וְחֻקָּתוֹ.
זָךְ שׁוֹכֵן מְעוֹנָה,
קוֹמֵם קְהַל מִי מָנָה.
קָרֵב נַהֵל נִטְעֵי כַנָּה,
פְּדוּיִם לְצִיּוֹן בְּרִנָּה.

Now we come to the close of our seder service.

Once again we have recited the age-old epic of Israel's liberation from bondage. Once again we have chanted our psalms of praise to God, the Redeemer of Israel and of all humankind. We have taken to heart the message of the Exodus. And we have rededicated ourselves to the cause of humanity's freedom from tyranny and oppression. As we have celebrated this festival tonight, so may we celebrate it, all of us together, next year again, in peace and in freedom.

All say in unison:

לְשָׁנָה הַבָּאָה בִּירוּשָׁלָיִם.

Lashanah haba'ah birushalayim.

May the coming year bring freedom to the oppressed, peace to Zion and Jerusalem, and the redemption of Israel and all humankind.

THE COUNTING OF THE OMER

Beginning on the second night of Passover, it is a tradition to count the days between Passover and Shavuot, the holiday that commemorates the giving of the Torah at Mount Sinai. The tradition is known as the "counting of the omer." Omer, meaning "sheaf," is a reference to the newly harvested sheaves of barley that our ancestors brought to the Temple as an offering on the second day of Passover. Counting the 49 days of the omer can increase our sense of anticipation and readiness as we shift our focus from freedom to Revelation.

בָּרוּךְ אַתָּה יְיָ אֱלֹהֵינוּ מֶלֶךְ הָעוֹלָם, אֲשֶׁר קִדְּשָׁנוּ בְּמִצְוֹתָיו וְצִוָּנוּ עַל סְפִירַת הָעוֹמֶר.

Baruch atah adonai eloheinu, melech ha'olam, asher kid'shanu b'mitzvotav v'tzivanu al s'firat ha'omer.

Praised are you, Adonai our God, Sovereign of the universe, who sanctifies us through your mitzvot and commands us to count the omer.

הַיּוֹם יוֹם אֶחָד לָעֹמֶר.

Hayom yom ehad la'omer.

Today is day one of the omer.

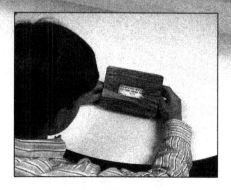

Using an omer counter

כמה
מעלות טובות
למקום עלינו

KAMAH MA'ALOT TOVOT LAMAKOM ALEINU!

HOW MANY ARE THE GOODLY FAVORS

GOD HAS BESTOWED UPON US!

HAD YOU GIVEN US CHILDREN

BUT NOT MADE THEM AS

BEAUTIFUL IN SPIRIT AS IN

FORM—THEY WOULD BE

ENOUGH.   DAYEINU!

HAD YOU MADE THEM AS

BEAUTIFUL IN SPIRIT AS IN

FORM BUT NOT PLACED LOVE AND

WISDOM IN THEIR HEARTS—THEY WOULD BE

ENOUGH. HAD YOU PLACED LOVE AND WISDOM IN

THEIR HEARTS BUT NOT SOWN HONOR AND RESPECT IN

THEIR MINDS—THEY WOULD BE ENOUGH. HAD YOU SOWN

HONOR AND RESPECT IN THEIR MINDS BUT NOT TAUGHT

THEM JUSTICE AND CHARITY—THEY WOULD BE ENOUGH.

AL ACHAT KAMAH V'CHAMAH TOVAH CH'FULA

UM'CHUPELET   LAMAKOM   ALEINU.

HOW MUCH GREATER IS OUR

INDEBTEDNESS

TO GOD

FOR DOUBLING AND

REDOUBLING THESE PRECIOUS GIFTS.

DEAR CHILDREN, KNOW THAT YOU ARE MORE THAN ENOUGH,

THAT YOU ARE A SIGN OF THE COVENANT AND A BLESSING TO OUR PEOPLE.

THESE PRECIOUS GIFTS   GILA GEVIRTZ